ENGLAND

ENGLAND

LITTLE BOOK OF FOOTBALL
TRIVIA & QUOTES

Written by Jon Reeves

Bath New York Singapore Hong Kong Cologne Delhi Melbourne

INTRODUCTION

From the World Cup success of 1966 to right up until now, England fans have enjoyed and endured many memorable moments. Some of the world's finest players have proudly worn the Three Lions badge on their chest, great managers have come and gone, and the famous Wembley Stadium has been knocked down and rebuilt.

With the domestic game in England booming as the Premiership continues to establish itself as the world's 'Premier League', the national team have struggled and often fallen short in recent years. But with the highly experienced and successful Italian coach, Fabio Capello at the helm, maybe the lions are ready to roar again.

The nation which brought the beautiful game to the world has been one of European football's most highly rated teams for years, and England's faithful fans have enjoyed many major tournaments, some enthralling football, satisfying victories and plenty of near misses along the way.

England's failure to qualify for the European Championship in 2008 left a proud footballing nation completely shell-shocked. Despite some solid performances at Wembley, the Three Lions struggled when it mattered most against group rivals, Croatia and Russia, and narrowly missed out after an agonising 3-2 Wembley win to the Croats.

Being an England football fan requires passion, nerves of steel and bucket loads of resilience. The team have kept supporters on the edge of their seats as vital qualifying games have come and gone, crucial World Cup and European Championship fixtures have been won and lost, and plenty of penalties have been scored and missed.

Geoff Hurst's famous hat-trick in 1966, the impressive campaign at Italia 1990 and the priceless 5-1 thrashing of Germany in their own backyard in 2001 – there have been plenty of Three Lions highs. But, inevitably, there have also been some lows, such as failing to qualify for the 1974 World Cup, the feelings of injustice following the loss to Argentina in 1986, and the disappointing 2-1 defeat to Russia in 2007.

Take a trip down memory lane, find out more about the men who made the headlines and get up to speed with the England squad. Grab an insight into the players' minds from some candid and entertaining quotes, and soak up the tantalizing trivia to become a walking 'Eng-cyclopaedia'.

"I knew I would never hit a better shot so long as I lived. The sound, the feel of the leather on leather was exactly right." – Sir Geoff Hurst recalling the third goal of his World Cup hat-trick in 1966, the goal which sealed victory for England

THE MANAGER

Fabio Capello has been a top-class football coach for 16 years and has won nine league titles, including seven in Italy and two in Spain. He also won the Champions League with AC Milan in 1994.

Capello's Clubs

Player: SPAL, Roma, Juventus, AC Milan.
Manager: AC Milan, Real Madrid, Roma, Juventus.

Playing as a midfielder, Fabio earned 32 international caps for Italy and notched up eight goals. He even scored the winning goal against England as the Italians beat the Three Lions for the first time at Wembley in 1973.

"Fabio is a very good man and manager. His record speaks very clear. He has won titles in Italy." – Sven-Goran Eriksson

Capello's first game as England boss was the friendly fixture against Switzerland at Wembley on 6 February 2008. England won the game 2-1 thanks to Jermaine Jenas and second-half substitute Shaun Wright-Phillips.

"I prefer to have a new experience, outside Italy. Between the national team and abroad, I choose England. For the language, the mentality. I believe I can do it. It is a dream of mine, something I have held for a long time." – Fabio Capello

Shaun Wright-Phillips celebrates with Steven Gerrard after scoring the winner against Switzerland.

"Fabio Capello is widely recognised as one of the world's finest coaches. He has achieved huge success wherever he has worked and has the respect of everyone in football." –
Sir Trevor Brooking

Fabio Capello watches on during his first game as England boss, against Switzerland at Wembley.

Fabio named the following as his first 11:	
David James	Jermaine Jenas
Wes Brown	Steven Gerrard
Ashley Cole	David Bentley
Matthew Upson	Wayne Rooney
Rio Ferdinand	Joe Cole
Gareth Barry	

YOUNGEST PLAYERS

When a young player breaks through into the England team and takes the international scene by storm, it's one of the most exciting sights in football. Many England players made their mark at the highest level at an early age.

Michael Owen debuted against Chile in 1998, aged 18 years and 59 days. He became England's youngest player of the 20th century.

Wayne Rooney made his debut against Australia in 2003 aged 17 years and 111 days.

Theo Walcott broke Rooney's record when he made his international debut against Hungary in 2006. Walcott was just 17 years and 75 days old.

However, Rooney still holds the record for England's youngest scorer. The Manchester United striker struck gold

against Macedonia in 2003 when he was just 17 years and 317 days old.

Michael Owen making his England debut against Chile at Wembley in 1998.

Did you know?
Micah Richards is England's youngest defender. The Manchester City man broke Rio Ferdinand's record when he made his debut against Holland in 2006 at the age of 18 years and 144 days.

Micah Richards clearing the ball during his debut outing against Holland.

Top Ten Youngest England Goalscorers

1 Wayne Rooney aged 17 years, 317 days on 6 September 2003 v Macedonia, EC Qualifier

2 Michael Owen aged 18 years, 163 days on 27 May 1998 v Morocco, King Hassan II Tournament

3 Tommy Lawton aged 19 years, 16 days on 22 October 1938 v Wales, Home Champ

4 Micah Richards aged 19 years, 75 days on 8 September 2007 v Israel, EC Qualifier

5 Jimmy Greaves aged 19 years, 85 days on 17 May 1959 v Peru, Friendly

6 Joseph Baker aged 19 years, 123 days on 18 November 1959 v N Ireland, Home Champ

7 James Brown aged 19 years, 202 days on 18 February 1882 v Ireland, Friendly

8 Duncan Edwards aged 19 years, 237 days on 26 May 1956 v West Germany, Friendly

9 Stanley Matthews aged 19 years, 239 days on 29 September 1934 v Wales, Home Champ

10 Jackie Robinson aged 19 years, 283 days on 20 May 1937 v Finland, Friendly

RECORD BREAKERS

Many England players have experienced the cut and thrust of a major international championship.

The following records state which tournament squads each player has been selected for, the number of games they've played and their goal tally.

Player	World Cup	European Championship	Games (incl. sub)	Goals
Scott Carson	2006	0	0	0
David James	2002, 2006	2004	4	0
Paul Robinson	2006	2004	5	0
Wayne Bridge	2002, 2006	2004	2	0
Wes Brown	2002	0	0	0
Sol Campbell	1998, 2002, 2006	1996, 2000, 2004	18	1
Ashley Cole	2002, 2006	2004	14	0
Rio Ferdinand	2002, 2006	0	10	1
Ledley King	0	2004	2	0
Phil Neville	2006	1996, 2000, 2004	5	0
David Beckham	1998, 2002, 2006	2000, 2004	20	3
Michael Carrick	2006	0	1	0
Joe Cole	2002, 2006	2004	6	1
Stewart Downing	2006	0	3	0
Kieron Dyer	2002	2004	4	0
Steven Gerrard	2006	2000, 2004	10	3
Owen Hargreaves	2002, 2006	2004	9	0
Jermaine Jenas	2006	0	0	0
Frank Lampard	2006	2004	9	3
Peter Crouch	2006	0	4	1
Emile Heskey	2002	2000, 2004	8	1
Michael Owen	1998, 2002, 2006	2000, 2004	19	6
Wayne Rooney	2006	2004	8	4

When he came on as a first-half substitute against Sweden at the 2006 World Cup, Sol Campbell was the first England player to appear at six major international tournaments.

Michael Owen is the only England player to score at four separate international tournaments: the 1998 and 2002 World Cups, and the 2000 and 2004 European Championships.

David Beckham's trademark long-range free kick against Ecuador at the 2006 meant he was the first Englishman to score at three separate World Cup finals.

None of the current England squad have ever appeared any further than the Quarter-finals of a major tournament, although Sol Campbell and Phil Neville were substitutes in the England team that went one step further at Euro 1996.

England are the only nation to lose all three World Cup shoot-outs they have been involved in. Italy had the same record until they beat France on penalties in 2006.

England have exited four of the last six major tournaments they have appeared in via the dreaded penalty shoot out.

Tournament:	Tournament:	Tournament:	Tournament:
1996 European Championship	1998 World Cup	2004 European Championship	2006 World Cup
Stage: Semi-final	Stage: Second round	Stage: Quarter-final	Stage: Quarter-final
Opponents: Germany	Opponents: Argentina	Opponents: Portugal	Opponents: Portugal
Score after 90 minutes: 1-1	Score after 90 minutes: 2-2	Score after 90 minutes: 1-1	Score after 90 minutes: 0-0
Score after extra-time: 1-1	Score after extra-time: 2-2	Score after extra-time: 2-2	Score after extra-time: 0-0
Penalty shoot out:	Penalty shoot out:	Penalty shoot out:	Penalty shoot out:
Germany won 6-5	Argentina won 4-3	Portugal won 6-5	Portugal won 3-1
Who missed for England?	Who missed for England?	Who missed for England?	Who missed for England?
Gareth Southgate	Paul Ince and David Batty	David Beckham and Darius Vassell	Frank Lampard, Steven Gerrard and Jamie Carragher

MAJOR HONOURS

A list of the England squad's honours.

Player	League Title	Cups	Total
David James	0	1 League Cup (1995)	1
Wayne Bridge	2 English Premier League (2005, 2006)	1 League Cup (2007) 1 FA Cup (2007)	4
Wes Brown	5 English Premier League (1999, 2000, 2001, 2003, 2007)	1 Champions League (1999) 2 FA Cups (1999, 2004) 1 League Cup (2006)	9
Sol Campbell	2 English Premier League (2002, 2004)	2 FA Cup (2002, 2005) 1 League Cup (1999)	5
Ashley Cole	2 English Premier League (2002, 2004)	4 FA Cups (2002, 2003, 2005 2007)	6
Rio Ferdinand	2 English Premier League (2003, 2007)	1 League Cup (2006)	3
Phil Neville	6 English Premier League (1996, 1997 1999, 2000, 2001, 2003)	3 FA Cups (1996, 1999, 2004) 1 Intercontinental Cup (1999)	10
David Beckham	6 English Premier League (1996, 1997 1999, 2000, 2001, 2003) 1 Spanish La Liga (2007)	2 FA Cups (1996, 1999)	11
Michael Carrick	1 English Premier League (2007)	0	1
Joe Cole	2 English Premier League (2005, 2006)	1 FA Cup (2007) 2 League Cups (2005, 2007)	5
Stewart Downing	0	1 League Cup (2004)	1
Steven Gerrard	0	1 Champions League (2005) 1 UEFA Cup (2001) 1 European Super Cup (2003) 2 FA Cups (2001, 2006) 2 League Cups (2001, 2003)	7

Player	League Title	Cups	Total
Owen Hargreaves	4 German Bundesliga (2001, 2003, 2005, 2006)	1 Champions League (2001) 1 Intercontinental Cup (2001) 3 German Cups (2003, 2005, 2006)	9
Frank Lampard	2 English Premier League (2005, 2006)	1 FA Cup (2007) 2 League Cups (2005, 2007)	5
Shaun Wright-Phillips	1 English Premier League (2006)	1 FA Cup (2007) 1 League Cup (2007)	3
Peter Crouch	0	1 FA Cup (2006)	1
Emile Heskey	0	1 UEFA Cup (2001) 1 European Super Cup (2001) 1 FA Cup (2001) 4 League Cup (1997, 2000, 2001 2003)	7
Michael Owen	0	1 UEFA Cup (2001) 1 European Super Cup (2001) 1 FA Cup (2001) 2 League Cups (2001, 2003)	5
Wayne Rooney	1 English Premier League (2007)	1 League Cup (2006)	2

"You just have to deal with it and, for me, that means playing my normal game. If you start doing things differently, that's when things can go wrong. I think, for example, that when a shot comes in, you have a bigger space if you have your hands spread to catch the ball rather than punching it. If you put your fists together and punch, you have a lot smaller area. If you spread your hands, you have a bigger area to catch it or at least take the sting out of the ball and palm it down." – Paul Robinson on preparing for the 2006 World Cup

ENGLAND GOALKEEPERS

David James

Club: Portsmouth
Previous clubs: Include Manchester City,
West Ham United
England debut: 29 March 1997,
against Mexico

David played in all of England's matches
during Euro 2004. James is the first
Portsmouth player to play for England
since Mark Hateley in 1984.

Scott Carson

Club: Aston Villa (on loan from Liverpool)
Previous clubs: Include Sheffield
Wednesday (on loan), Leeds United
England debut: 16 November 2007,
against Austria

Scott's younger brother, Grant Carson, is
also a goalkeeper, for Carlisle United.
Scott Carson previously held the record
for most appearances for the England
Under-21 side, with 29 in total.

Robert Green

Club: West Ham United
Previous club: Norwich City
England debut: 31 May 2005,
against Colombia

Green was called into the England
squad for the first time for the friendly
in Sweden in March 2004, before
making his England debut in May 2005,
coming on to replace David James at
half-time.

Chris Kirkland

Club: Wigan Athletic
Previous clubs: West Bromwich Albion (on
loan), Liverpool, Coventry City
England debut: 16 August 2006,
against Greece

When Chris Kirkland made his England
debut in 2006, his father was a happy man
for more than one reason. Years earlier, he
had placed a bet that his son would play
for the senior team at odds of 100-1.

David James in England action against Switzerland in 2008.

"I am sure Mr Capello has his own ideas – but I'll enjoy it, train well and hope to impress. That's all I can do. But deep down I hope I get the nod, and if I do it will be a great boost for me. I'm not aiming to be there just to make up the numbers."
– Chris Kirkland

Paul Robinson at the 2006 World Cup.

Paul Robinson

Club: Tottenham Hotspur
Previous club: Leeds United
England debut: 12 February 2003, against Australia

Spurs goalkeeper Paul Robinson has earned over 40 caps for his country and been a consistent custodian in the Premier League.

ENGLAND DEFENDERS

Rio Ferdinand

Club: Manchester United
Previous clubs: Leeds United, AFC
Bournemouth (on loan), West Ham United
England debut: 15 November 1997,
against Cameroon

In the ten World Cup finals matches Rio
has played for England, the Three Lions
kept seven clean sheets and conceded just
four goals.

Micah Richards

Club: Manchester City
Previous club: None
England debut: 15 November 2006,
against Holland

At international level, Micah has been
capped for the Under 16s, Under 19s and
earned his first cap with the Under-21s
against Moldova in August 2006.

John Terry

Club: Chelsea
Previous club: Nottingham Forest (on
loan)
England debut: 3 June 2003, against Serbia
& Montenegro

JT was first named as England captain
in August 2006. His brother Paul is also
a professional footballer and is currently
on the books of Leyton Orient.

Ashley Cole

Club: Chelsea
Previous clubs: Arsenal, Crystal Palace
(on loan)
England debut: 28 March 2001, against
Albania

Ashley is one of the finest left-backs in
the world due to his tight defensive
displays, pace and creativity going forward.
He was voted into the UEFA Team of the
Tournament at Euro 2004.

Ledley King

Club: Tottenham Hotspur
Previous clubs: None
England debut: 27 March 2002,
against Italy

Ledley holds the record for the fastest goal
ever scored in a Premier League match.
He scored after just ten seconds against
Bradford City in 2000.

Wes Brown

Club: Manchester United
Previous club: None
England debut: 28 April 1999,
against Hungary

Despite being a regular in the England
squad for almost a decade, Wes has
never featured in a fixture at a major
international championship.

England's Group for the 2010 World Cup Qualifying Campaign

Group 6

Croatia
England
Ukraine
Belarus
Kazakhstan
Andorra

"John has all the attributes an international captain needs – leadership, authority, courage, ability, tactical awareness and a total refusal to accept second-best." – Steve McClaren on John Terry

ENGLAND MIDFIELDERS

Frank slotting home a penalty under extreme pressure in England's home defeat to Croatia in 2007.

Frank Lampard

Club: Chelsea
Previous clubs: West Ham United, Swansea City (on loan)
England debut: 10 October 1999, against Belgium

In 2005 Lampard was a runner-up to Brazilian maestro Ronaldinho twice, firstly in the European Footballer of the Year award and secondly in the FIFA World Player of the Year Award.

Steven Gerrard

Club: Liverpool
Previous clubs: None
England debut: 31 May 2000, against Ukraine

Steven was named England's vice-captain in August 2006 and he captained the Three Lions for Fabio Capello's first game in charge in February 2008.

Owen Hargreaves

Club: Manchester United
Previous club: Bayern Munich
England debut: 15 August 2001,
against Holland

"He's (Fabio Capello) had so much success as a club manager, I think that he will be a success with us. We've got great players, we've got a great manager, so there are no reasons why he can't do it..." – Owen Hargreaves

Other Midfielders

Gareth Barry
David Beckham
David Bentley
Joe Cole
Jermaine Jenas

*Did you know?
The last five Official England
Fans' Players of the Year have
all been midfielders.*

Michael Carrick

Club: Manchester United
Previous clubs: Tottenham Hotspur,
Birmingham City (on loan), Swindon Town
(on loan), West Ham United
England debut: 25 May 2001, against
Mexico

*Owen Hargreaves
in England action
against Switzerland at
Wembley in 2008.*

Year	Player
2003	David Beckham
2004	Frank Lampard
2005	Frank Lampard
2006	Owen Hargreaves
2007	Steven Gerrard

ENGLAND STRIKERS

England's Euro 2008 Qualifying Campaign

2 September 2006	Andorra	H	W	5-0
6 September 2006	Macedonia	A	W	1-0
7 October 2006	Macedonia	H	D	0-0
11 October 2006	Croatia	A	L	0-2
24 March 2007	Israel	A	D	0-0
28 March 2007	Andorra	A	W	3-0
6 June 2007	Estonia	A	W	3-0
8 September 2007	Israel	H	W	3-0
12 September 2007	Russia	H	W	3-0
13 October 2007	Estonia	H	W	3-0
17 October 2007	Russia	A	L	1-2
21 November 2007	Croatia	H	L	2-3

Top of Final Group E Table

Team	Pld	W	D	L	Pts
Croatia	12	9	2	1	29
Russia	12	7	3	2	24
England	12	7	2	3	23

"As an Englishman, you want the best man for the job who is going to try and help us win trophies. And personally I think he is the best man. Hopefully we can win something for him and help him become a legend for England." – Wayne Rooney on Fabio Capello

Michael Owen

Club: Newcastle United
Previous clubs: Real Madrid, Liverpool
England debut: 11 February 1998, against Chile

Michael was named European Footballer of the Year in 2001, the same year that he claimed UEFA, FA and League Cup medals at club level with Liverpool.

Michael Owen slams home another vital goal, as England beat Russia 3-0 in 2007.

Wayne Rooney

Club: Manchester United
Previous club: Everton
England debut: 12 February 2003,
against Australia

Rooney became England's youngest ever
scorer in 2003. He was just 17 years and
317 days old.

Jermain Defoe

Club: Portsmouth
Previous clubs: Tottenham Hotspur,
AFC Bournemouth, West Ham United
(both on loan)
England debut: 31 March 2004, against
Sweden

Jermain scored in ten successive
League games when he was on loan at
Bournemouth.

*"He is a manager who knows
what he wants. He has an aura
about him. When he walks into
a room everyone takes notice.
That is something you need from
an England manager." – Peter
Crouch on Fabio Capello*

Peter Crouch

Club: Liverpool
Previous clubs: Include Southampton,
Norwich City (on loan), Aston Villa
England debut: 31 May 2005, against
Colombia

At 6ft 7in Peter is the tallest player to
ever play for the Three Lions.

Top Ten Youngest England Captains

1 Bobby Moore aged 22 years, 46 days on 29 May 1963 v Czechoslovakia, Friendly
2 Tinsley Lindley aged 22 years, 99 days on 4 Feb 1888 v Wales, Home Champ
3 Michael Owen aged 22 years, 123 days on 17 Apr 2002 v Paraguay, Friendly
4 Cuthbert Ottaway aged 22 years, 133 days on 30 Nov 1872 v Scotland, Friendly
5 William Rawson aged 22 years, 140 days on 3 March 1877 v Scotland, Friendly
6 Percy Melmoth Walters aged 22 years, 164 days on 13 Mar 1886 v Ireland, Home Champ
7 Stan Cullis aged 22 years, 209 days on 24 May 1939 v Romania, Friendly
8 Basil Patchitt aged 22 years, 281 days on 21 May 1923 v Sweden, Friendly
9 William Moon aged 22 years, 282 days on 6 Apr 1891 v Scotland, Home Champ
10 Gilbert Oswald Smith aged 23 years, 102 days on 7 Mar 1896 v Ireland, Home Champ

THE WORLD CUP

From glorious campaigns which unite the whole country, like Euro 1996, Italia 1990 and, of course, the 1966 World Cup win, to the disappointing displays and feelings of injustice that have left a bitter taste in the mouth, such as the Euro 2004 exit and Maradona's infamous 'hand of God' – throughout it all, England have played their part in some of football's most memorable moments.

Year	Hosts	England's Performance	Winners
1930	Uruguay	Did not enter	Uruguay
1934	Italy	Did not enter	Italy
1938	France	Did not enter	Italy
1950	Brazil	Round 1	Uruguay
1954	Switzerland	Quarter-finals	West Germany
1958	Sweden	Round 1	Brazil
1962	Chile	Quarter-finals	Brazil
1966	England	Winners	England
1970	Mexico	Quarter-finals	Brazil
1974	West Germany	Did not qualify	West Germany
1978	Argentina	Did not qualify	Argentina
1982	Spain	Round 2	Italy
1986	Mexico	Quarter-finals	Argentina
1990	Italy	Semi-finals	West Germany
1994	USA	Did not qualify	Brazil
1998	France	Round 2	France
2002	Japan & South Korea	Quarter-finals	Brazil
2006	Germany	Quarter-finals	Italy

The hosts of the World Cup have also been the eventual winners on six occasions, including England's 1966 success.

As three-time winners, Uruguay, Italy and Brazil would have been presented with the Jules Rimet trophy to keep, had they won the World Cup in 1966.

Brazil did manage to get their hands on the trophy four years later, after claiming the 1970 title.

Before the 1966 World Cup in England the Jules Rimet trophy was stolen from an exhibition. Thankfully it was later recovered by a dog named Pickles.

Only two players scored for England at the 1950 finals, Wilf Mannion, the Middlesbrough striker, and Stan Mortensen, the Blackpool centre-forward.

England and West Germany line-up for the 1966 World Cup Final at Wembley.

WORLD CUP HOT SHOTS

The table at the bottom of the page lists England's top scorers at each World Cup they've played in, and the winner of the FIFA's golden boot for each tournament's top scorer.

Bobby Moore and Martin Peters celebrating at Wembley in 1966.

Steven Gerrard (centre), scoring in the World Cup group game against Sweden in 2006.

Year	England's Top Scorer	Tournament's Top Scorer	Country
1950	Wilf Mannion & Stan Mortensen – 1 goal	Ademir – 9 goals	Brazil
1958	Derek Kevan – 2 goals	Just Fontaine – 13 goals	France
1962	Ron Flowers – 2 goals	Garrincha - All scored 4 goals	Brazil
		Vava	Brazil
		Lionel Sanchez	Chile
		Drazen Jerkovic	Yugoslavia
		Florian Albert	Hungary
		Valentin Ivanov	USSR
1966	Geoff Hurst – 4 goals	Eusebio – 9 goals	Portugal
1970	Allan Clarke – 1 goal	Gerd Muller – 9 goals	W Germany
	Geoff Hurst – 1 goal		
	Alan Mullery – 1 goal		
	Martin Peters – 1 goal		
1982	Trevor Francis & Bryan Robson – 2 goals	Paulo Rossi – 6 goals	Italy
1986	Gary Lineker – 6 goals	Gary Lineker – 6 goals	England
1990	Gary Lineker – 4 goals	Salvatore Schillaci – 6 goals	Italy
1998	Alan Shearer & Michael Owen – 2 goals	Davor Suker – 6 goals	Croatia
2002	Michael Owen – 2 goals	Ronaldo – 8 goals	Brazil
2006	Steven Gerrard – 2 goals	Miroslav Klose – 5 goals	Germany

Gary Lineker, England's top scorer for two World Cup tournaments, in action against West Germany in 1990.

Michael Owen is the youngest player to appear for England at a World Cup. He was just 18 years and 183 days old when he came on as a second-half substitute against Romania at France 1998. Eleven days later, in England's contest against Colombia, he became the youngest player to ever start for the Three Lions in a World Cup at 18 years and 194 days.

Englands World Cup XI
1. Gordon Banks
2. George Cohen
3. Stuart Pearce
4. Nobby Stiles
5. Bobby Moore
6. Terry Butcher
7. Alan Ball
8. Paul Gascoigne
9. Gary Lineker
10. Geoff Hurst
11. Bobby Charlton

Did you know?
Teddy Sheringham holds the record for most substitute appearances for England. The much travelled striker was brought on 21 times during his Three Lions career.

A Record of the Biggest World Cup Wins	
Year	Result
1982	Hungary 10 – 1 El Salvador
1954	Hungary 9 – 0 South Korea
1974	Yugoslavia 9 – 0 Zaire
1938	Sweden 8 – 0 Cuba
1950	Uruguay 8 – 0 Bolivia
2002	Germany 8 – 0 Saudi Arabia

Teddy Sheringham (left) after coming on as a substitute against Greece in 2001.

1966 WORLD CUP

It was England's turn to host the World Cup in 1966, which ensured automatic qualification for the Three Lions.

England 0	Uruguay	0
England 2	Mexico	0
England 2	France	0
England 1	Argentina	0
England 2	Portugal	1

The new manager, Alf Ramsey, declared that England would win the Jules Rimet trophy, showing supreme confidence in the players and his own ability.

Despite the excitement and expectation in England, the team started slowly. The light blue shirts of the Uruguayans massed in defence throughout the opening game of the tournament, and England could not find a way through.

The game against Mexico started in a similar way, until a Bobby Charlton thunderbolt and a Roger Hunt clincher. The often unsung hero, Hunt, followed with two goals against France, and England marched into the Quarter-finals.

The games were getting tougher and Argentina continually frustrated England, until Antonio Rattin, the Argentinian captain, was sent off. It took a late header from Geoff Hurst to secure a place in the Semi-finals against Portugal.

Two trademark goals from Bobby Charlton set England on the march, and the defence withstood Portugal's late rally and Eusebio's penalty. Ramsey's men had made the Final!

STAR PLAYERS
Geoff Hurst

England's hat-trick hero in the Final came into the side at the Quarter-final stage, following an injury to Jimmy Greaves. Hurst scored the winning goal against Argentina and kept his place in the team for the Final, even with Greaves back to full fitness. Hurst was capped 49 times, scoring 24 goals.

Bobby Moore

If Hurst was the star of the World Cup Final, Moore was the man of the Finals, hardly putting a foot wrong throughout the tournament. Moore played 108 matches, 90 as captain, a record which he shares with Billy Wright.

Bobby Charlton

The driving force of the England team throughout the 1960s, Bobby Charlton could hit a ball with great power using either foot and was a tireless worker playing in an advanced midfield role. He scored plenty of vital goals for his country including some crucial strikes during the 1966 World Cup.

Gordon Banks

Probably England's best ever goalkeeper, Gordon Banks was in fine form during the 1966 World Cup. Banks was great at commanding his area and claiming high crosses. He represented his country on 73 occasions.

1966 England World Cup Squad	
Gordon Banks	Ronald Springett
George Cohen	Peter Bonetti
Ray Wilson	Jimmy Armfield
Nobby Stiles	Gerry Byrne
Jack Charlton	Martin Peters
Bobby Moore	Ron Flowers
Alan Ball	Norman Hunter
Jimmy Greaves	Terry Paine
Bobby Charlton	Ian Callaghan
Geoff Hurst	Roger Hunt
John Connelly	George Eastham

1966 WORLD CUP FINAL

The Final was played at Wembley Stadium on 30 July 1966.

Could Alf Ramsey deliver what he'd promised, a first World Cup for his country? England began nervously, and Helmut Haller pounced on an error to put the West Germans ahead. Hurst equalised with another header from a Bobby Moore free-kick. With 12 minutes to go, Martin Peters smashed in a loose ball to make it 2-1 to England.

The Three Lions were almost home, but then, deep into injury-time, a disputed free-kick was awarded, and Wolfgang Weber scored the equaliser.

Martin Peters celebrates scoring England's second goal of the 1966 Final.

"We were the world champions, which was a fantastic feeling. I knew that life for me would never be the same again."
– Sir Bobby Charlton

Inspirational captain Bobby Moore holds the Jules Rimet trophy aloft.

"I have to admit that I had a bit of sympathy for the Germans. They genuinely believed the ball had not crossed the line, and they may be right." – Sir Geoff Hurst

It would be the first World Cup Final to go to extra-time. The players summoned up the required energy to re-take the led. A probing run from Alan Ball down the right lead to a deep cross and shot from Hurst. The ball cannoned off the underside of the bar and was controversially declared a goal. The Germans protested but the officials were having none of it. England were 3-2 up.

With seconds of the game remaining, Hurst removed all doubt by rifling home a shot into the roof of the net, following a perfectly measured long-ball from Bobby Moore. It was the classic hat-trick – header, right foot, left foot – and remains the only one scored in a World Cup Final.

Ramsey's prediction had come to pass. He had made a sound defence even more solid, and given the team more weight and bite in midfield, without sacrificing too much attacking flair. The team dubbed the 'wingless wonders' had brought home the World Cup, with a win of 4-2.

First Round: Group 1							
Team	Pts	Pld	W	D	L	GF	GA
England	5	3	2	1	0	4	0
Uruguay	4	3	1	2	0	2	1
Mexico	2	3	0	2	1	1	3
France	1	3	0	1	2	2	5

1970 WORLD CUP

As World Cup holders, England set out to defend their title in Mexico in 1970.

Their preparations were thrown into chaos during a warm-up tour when skipper Bobby Moore was falsely accused of jewellery theft in Colombia and arrested.

When the tournament kicked off, the team didn't let the furore surrounding their captain affect them. Victories over solid European opposition made sure they reached the Quarter-finals.

England's most impressive performance came in their second group match against Brazil. Ramsey's men were beaten 1-0, despite Gordon Banks displaying one of the finest saves ever seen and Bobby

England 1 Romania 0	
England 0 Brazil 1	
England 1 Czechoslovakia 0	
England 2 West Germany 3 (aet)	

Moore's imperious defending keeping Pelé quiet for large periods. A sharp Jairzinho goal and a miss by Jeff Astle ensured that Brazil edged the victory.

England eagerly awaited the chance of revenge in the Final, but it was not to be. The Quarter-final against West Germany seemed to be going in England's favour, as they cruised to a 2-0 lead.

Then Ramsey took off Bobby Charlton – in what turned out to be his last appearance for his country – to rest him for the Semi-final. Franz Beckenbauer, freed from marking Charlton, inspired a recovery as both he and Uwe Seeler scored to pull the scores level. Peter Bonetti, a replacement in goal for Gordon Banks, who was stricken with food poisoning, struggled as the Germans forced extra-time. Gerd Muller grabbed the winner and ended England's defence of their title.

"I still get excited when I see the save on TV; it's been shown so many times, and of course it's nice when people talk about it being the greatest save ever." –
Gordon Banks

Two of the game's greats, Bobby Moore and Pelé, shake hands and embrace at the end of England's 1-0 defeat to Brazil in 1970.

Gordon Banks is arguably the finest goalkeeper England has ever produced.

"I thought it was a goal. There's one take on TV where you can see that I started to jump, to say 'Goal…' then I say, 'Oh…' It was a fantastic save and it shows that sometimes it's not just goals that people remember." – *Pelé*

England sealed qualification for the Mexico Finals after winning a group which included Northern Ireland and Romania.

England 0 Portugal 1
England 0 Morocco 0
England 3 Poland 0
England 3 Paraguay 0
England 1 Argentina 2

On reaching the tournament, England made things difficult for themselves. They lost to Portugal in the opening match and drew with Morocco. In this game, Ray Wilkins became the first English player to be sent off in a World Cup. A hat-trick from Gary Lineker against Poland helped him on his way to winning the Golden Boot.

"It wasn't the 'hand of God'. It was the hand of a rascal. God had nothing to do with it." – Sir Bobby Robson

England went forward to face Paraguay in the Azteca Stadium. Two more goals from Lineker and one from Peter Beardsley put them into the Quarter-finals.

In a pulsating match, Maradona's 'hand of God' goal was followed by a magnificent solo effort by the talented Argentinian player to make it 2-0. Then manager Bobby Robson brought on John Barnes.

"The goal was scored a little bit by the hand of God and a little bit by the head of Maradona." – Diego Maradona

Barnes terrorised the Argentine defence, and made one (and nearly another) opportunity for Lineker to score. England came within a hairbreadth of extra-time. Yet England were out, and Argentina went on to lift the trophy.

"No one could believe it. Everyone ran up to the referee, I ran up to him… it was just incredible that the goal was given. It's still hard to believe."
– Peter Shilton

Did you know?
There were two players with the same first and last names in the 1986 World Cup squad. Defenders Gary Stevens of Everton and Gary Stevens of Spurs were in Bobby Robson's 22.

Diego Maradona executes his infamous 'hand of God' goal, leaving England players and fans in disbelief.

1990 WORLD CUP

Qualifying second behind Sweden in a rather lacklustre fashion did not give England great hopes for Italy, particularly after the disappointing 1988 European Championship campaign.

England 1 Ireland 1
England 0 Netherlands 0
England 1 Egypt 0
England 1 Belgium 0 (aet)
England 3 Cameroon 2 (aet)
England 1 West Germany 1 (aet: West Germany won 4-3 on penalties)
England 1 Italy 2 (Third Place Play-off)

After an early goal by Gary Lineker, England faded in the first group match against Ireland and drew 1-1.

The following match against the European champions, Holland, was a distinct improvement, with Paul Gascoigne beginning to make a name for himself as a quality player.

A forgettable game against Egypt was enlivened by a rare Mark Wright-headed goal, and England moved into the last 16. There, a cat-and-mouse match with the Belgians was finally won when David Platt volleyed from a lofted Gascoigne free-kick, just as extra-time expired. Another goal from Platt and a brace of Lineker penalties were enough to see off the spirited challenge from Cameroon in the Quarter-finals.

West Germany awaited England for the Semi-finals in Turin. It was a close game, with few clear chances to either side, until Andreas Brehme's free kick was wickedly deflected via Paul Parker's back

"The instant the ref waved that yellow card in front of my nose, I knew that no matter the result, my World Cup was over..." – Paul Gascoigne

> *"I watched Italia 1990 with my mum, dad and brother, leaping around when the penalties were on."*
> *– Steven Gerrard*

past Peter Shilton. But England fought back and Gary Lineker, surrounded by German defenders, swivelled to slide home the equaliser.

Chris Waddle hit the post from a distance in extra-time and Paul Gascoigne was booked, meaning he'd miss the Final if England got there. As the tears of disappointment and desperation rolled down Gazza's face, a legend was born.

England continued to press for a winner, but with the Germans defending in numbers, extra-time was soon up and the teams were set for

the dramatic denouement of penalties. The Germans didn't miss, but England stars Waddle and Stuart Pearce did, and England crashed out of the World Cup.

The third and fourth play-off match was against Italy, but England were defeated and finished in fourth place.

Paul 'Gazza' Gascoigne keeps the ball under his spell during the 1990 World Cup Semi-final with West Germany.

OTHER WORLD CUPS

Being drawn with Germany in the 2002 qualifying group for Japan and Korea was tough enough – losing 1-0 in the last match at the old Wembley Stadium was devastating.

Keegan resigned as manager, and Sven-Goran Eriksson took over. Results stabilised, until England went to Munich and chalked up a memorable 5-1 victory. Even then, it needed David Beckham's last-minute free-kick in the final fixture against Greece to ensure automatic qualification.

In the second tournament match, Argentina conceded a penalty which Beckham hammered home.

England 1 Sweden 1
England 1 Argentina 0
England 0 Nigeria 0
England 3 Denmark 0
England 1 Brazil 2

A stalemate against Nigeria took England into the last 16, where they outplayed Denmark with goals from Rio Ferdinand, Michael Owen and Emile Heskey.

Owen snatched the lead against Brazil in the Quarter-finals. But then, just before half-time, a slick passing move saw Rivaldo slide the ball home. In the second half, Ronaldinho's long-range free-kick deceived Seaman and, although the Brazilian was soon sent off, England slumped out of the competition.

David Beckham (top) and Danny Mills (right) mob Michael Owen after his opening goal against Brazil at the 2002 World Cup.

Qualification in 2006 was relatively straightforward, until Northern Ireland hustled England out of their stride and David Healy's goal grabbed a famous 1-0 win in front of an emotional Belfast crowd.

England 1 Paraguay 0
England 2 Trinidad & Tobago 0
England 2 Sweden 2
England 1 Ecuador 0
England 0 Portugal 0 (aet:
Portugal won 3-1 on penalties)

Fortunately, England managed to beat Austria and Poland at home to ensure they topped the group.

An early strike in the first game against Paraguay was not followed up, and it took the last ten minutes before goals from Peter Crouch and Steven Gerrard put away the Trinidadians.

Excellent goals from Joe Cole and Gerrard seemed to have ended the Swedish jinx, but England conceded a late equaliser.

A scrappy game against Ecuador was won by another Beckham free-kick, before Rooney was sent off against Portugal, and England were compelled to mount a rearguard action. Nevertheless, with Owen Hargreaves putting in a heroic all-action performance, England had a few chances to win the match, before losing again on penalties.

"I was sure these players could get to the Final and we should have done it. I'm sorry for the fans, who have been fantastic, that we couldn't give them a final." – Sven-Goran Eriksson

EUROPEAN CHAMPIONSHIP

Germany have clocked up the most appearances in the European Championship. The three-time champions have participated at ten separate tournaments.

The overall top scorer in the tournament's history is French legend Michel Platini with nine goals. Next on the list is England's former captain Alan Shearer with a tally of seven.

The Henri Delaunay trophy, which is awarded to the winner of the European Football Championship, is named in honour of the first General Secretary of UEFA. Henri came up with the idea of a European Championship, but died five years prior to the first tournament in 1960.

For the 2008 tournament, the trophy has been slightly remodelled and

Year	Hosts	England's Performance	Winners
1960	France	Did not enter	USSR
1964	Spain	Did not qualify	Spain
1968	Italy	Semi-finals (finished third)	Italy
1972	Belgium	Did not qualify	West Germany
1976	Yugoslavia	Did not qualify	Czechoslovakia
1980	Italy	Round 1	West Germany
1984	France	Did not qualify	France
1988	West Germany	Round 1	Holland
1992	Sweden	Round 1	Denmark
1996	England	Semi-finals	Germany
2000	Holland & Belgium	Round 1	France
2004	Portugal	Quarter-finals	Greece

increased in size. The trophy, which is made of sterling silver, now weighs eight kilograms and is 60 centimetres tall.

Euro 2004 winners, Greece, had not won a single match at the Championship prior to their success.

Paul Gascoigne celebrates hitting the target against Scotland at the 1996 European Championship.

"I want to tell the people in Greece that it is not a dream – we are the champions of Europe. There may have been some teams that were better with the ball, but in every sport, strategy also plays a significant role ... the team developed and improved as the tournament went on." - Triumphant Greek coach Otto Rehhagel

EURO HOT SHOTS

Year	England's Top Scorer	Tournament's Top Scorer	Their Country
1968	Geoff Hurst & Bobby Charlton – 1 goal	Dragan Dzajic	Yugoslavia
1980	Trevor Brooking, Ray Wilkins Tony Woodcock – 1 goal	Klaus Allofs – 3 goals	West Germany
1988	Bryan Robson & Tony Adams – 1 goal	Marco Van Basten – 5 goals	Holland
1992	David Platt – 1 goal	Henrik Larsson, Karlheinz Riedle, Dennis Bergkamp & Tomas Brolin – 3 goals	Sweden Germany Holland Sweden
1996	Alan Shearer – 5 goals	Alan Shearer – 5 goals	England
2000	Alan Shearer – 2 goals	Patrick Kluivert & Savo Milosevic – 5 goals	Holland Yugoslavia
2004	Wayne Rooney – 4 goals	Milan Baros – 5 goals	Czech Republic

"Historically, the host nations do well in Euro 2000." – Trevor Brooking

Alan Shearer wheels away in distinctive fashion after giving England the lead against Germany at Euro 1996.

When Wayne Rooney scored in the group stages against Switzerland on 17 June 2004, he became the youngest ever player to score at a European Championship. The record was broken by Swiss striker Johan Vonlanthen just four days later when he scored against France.

David Beckham (right) congratulates Wayne Rooney after he scored against the Swiss at Euro 2004.

"I don't remember anyone of his age having this sort of impact on a major tournament since Pelé in 1958. That was the World Cup in Sweden. He drops into midfield and he can take the ball, hold it, turn with it. He seems to be a complete football player." – Sven-Goran Eriksson on Rooney's impact at Euro 2004

1968 EUROPEAN CHAMPIONSHIP

The Home International Championship was the qualifying group for a place in the 1968 Quarter-finals, and a famous win for Scotland at Wembley in 1967 put England's participation in jeopardy.

However, a defeat for Scotland by George Best's Northern Ireland team meant England needed only a draw in Glasgow the following year, and a goal from Martin Peters ensured they got it.

Reigning European champions Spain met the World Cup holders over two legs, and England won both games: 1-0 at Wembley with Bobby Charlton as the scorer, and 2-1 in Madrid through Peters and Norman Hunter.

The Semi-final in Florence was a bad-tempered affair. Alan Mullery was sent off after Dzajic's goal against the run of play had given Yugoslavia

the lead. The resulting play-off was a meaningless anti-climax, although Bobby Charlton and George Hurst sealed a 2-0 win against the USSR.

England 0 Yugoslavia 1
England 2 USSR 0
(Third Place Play-off)

Did you know?
During the 1968 tournament,
Alan Mullery became the first
England player to be sent
off in an international when
he was red-carded against
Yugoslavia.

Alan Mullery walks off the field after receiving his marching orders in 1968.

44

Sir Alf Ramsey (left) was still at the helm as England took on Europe's finest, two years after the World Cup triumph.

1988 & 1992 EUROPEAN CHAMPIONSHIPS

England gave powerful performances against Turkey (8-0 at Wembley), Northern Ireland and Yugoslavia (4-1 in Belgrade) in the 1988 European Championship. They advanced to West Germany with high expectations.

Once there, these hopes were soon deflated. Ireland hustled them to defeat through Ray Houghton's header and, although England improved markedly against the Dutch, Marco Van Basten's imperious hat-trick overrode Bryan Robson's brave goal. With no chance of making the Semi-finals, the match against the Russians held little attraction.

England 0 Ireland 1
England 1 Netherlands 3
England 1 USSR 3

England's 'Captain Marvel', Bryan Robson, was one of the few shining lights of the 1988 European Championship.

In the 1992 qualifiers, England sneaked through after two draws against their nemesis, Jack Charlton's Ireland, and thanks to Lineker's late equaliser in Poland.

Public patience with Graham Taylor was wearing thin after two more draws, one against the shock winners of the tournament, and a defeat against the hosts, Sweden, after Platt had given England an early lead.

Did you know?
The eventual winners, Denmark, only took part in the tournament because Yugoslavia were prevented from playing as a result of sanctions placed upon them due to the war in their country. The Danes had finished behind Yugoslavia in their qualifying group.

The energetic David Platt celebrates scoring England's only goal of the 1992 European Championship in Sweden.

| England 0 Denmark 0 |
| England 0 France 0 |
| England 1 Sweden 2 |

"Shearer could be at 100 per cent fitness, but not peak fitness." – Graham Taylor

1996 EUROPEAN CHAMPIONSHIP

As hosts, England were spared the trials of qualification, but there was a downside to this – Terry Venables had never managed England in a competitive match. The team appeared well-organised and tough to beat, but only intermittently capable of blowing teams away. So it proved...

Switzerland grabbed a late penalty to equalise Alan Shearer's commanding strike and David Seaman had to save another penalty before Shearer's header and Paul Gascoigne's wonder goal saw off Scotland.

Then came the explosion as the Three Lions out-played Holland on a famous Wembley night, exhibiting some fantastic football, with the score finishing 4-1 to the hosts.

In the Quarter-final, the enormously impressive Spanish side came to Wembley and almost ran the show for 120 minutes. Unusually, England, and in particular Stuart Pearce, earned redemption through penalties. Was football coming home?

The Semi-final with Germany was preceded by an ominous thunderstorm. England played almost as well as they did against the Dutch, but without being able to translate their superiority into goals, after Shearer's potentially devastating opener. The game ended with penalties again, and it was another defeat for England with Gareth Southgate the fall guy this time around.

England 1 Switzerland 1
England 2 Scotland 0
England 4 Netherlands 1
England 0 Spain 0 (aet: England won 4-2 on penalties)
England 1 Germany 1 (aet: Germany won 6-5 on penalties)

England's Full Euro 1996 Squad	
Player	**Club**
1. David Seaman	Arsenal
2. Gary Neville	Manchester United
3. Stuart Pearce	Nottingham Forest
4. Paul Ince	Inter Milan
5. Tony Adams	Arsenal
6. Gareth Southgate	Aston Villa
7. David Platt	Arsenal
8. Paul Gascoigne	Glasgow Rangers
9. Alan Shearer	Blackburn Rovers
10. Teddy Sheringham	Tottenham Hotspur
11. Darren Anderton	Tottenham Hotspur
12. Steve Howey	Newcastle United
13. Tim Flowers	Blackburn Rovers
14. Nicky Barmby	Middlesbrough
15. Jamie Redknapp	Liverpool
16. Sol Campbell	Tottenham Hotspur
17. Steve McManaman	Liverpool
18. Les Ferdinand	Newcastle United
19. Philip Neville	Manchester United
20. Steve Stone	Nottingham Forest
21. Robbie Fowler	Liverpool
22. Ian Walker	Tottenham Hotspur

A vital part of the 1996 squad, Stuart Pearce displaying the passion and desire he was famed for.

2004 EUROPEAN CHAMPIONSHIP

Turkey, World Cup Semi-finalists in 2002, were the main rivals for England in a group that also included Slovakia, Macedonia and Liechtenstein, in the 2004 European Championship.

After beating the Turks 2-0 at Sunderland, another win against Liechtenstein meant England needed to gain at least one point in Istanbul to qualify. Despite Beckham's missed penalty, a composed yet battling performance saw England draw 0-0.

Championship holders France were also kept at arm's length for much of the first match, and Frank Lampard scored just before half-time to secure the lead. The result looked certain until two late Zidane strikes, from a free-kick and a penalty, snatched victory. But England responded well with convincing wins over Switzerland, in which two goals came from Wayne Rooney and one from Steven Gerrard, and Croatia, with Paul Scholes, Lampard and Rooney (two) as the scorers.

England 1 France 2
England 3 Switzerland 0
England 4 Croatia 2
England 2 Portugal 2 (aet: Portugal won 6-5 on penalties)

Did you know?
England were the joint top goalscorers at Euro 2004. Sven-Goran Eriksson's men and the Czech Republic both scored ten times.

The young Rooney was fast becoming the star of the Championship.

After Owen had given England the lead against the hosts, disaster struck as Rooney was carried off after a late challenge. England lost momentum, but even so, it took a late equaliser from Portugal and a crucially disallowed goal from Campbell before it went to penalties. Heartbreakingly, the Portuguese goalkeeper Ricardo applied the coup de grace after Darius Vassell's miss.

Sol Campbell, Ashley Cole, Frank Lampard and Wayne Rooney were all voted into the official UEFA Team of the Tournament.

Rooney adds to his tally with a venomous effort against Croatia in the final group match.

EURO FAST FACTS

Most Caps	Most Goals
Gary Neville 11	Alan Shearer 7
Tony Adams 9	Wayne Rooney 4
Alan Shearer 9	Frank Lampard 3
Stuart Pearce 8	Teddy Sheringham 2
Sol Campbell 8	Paul Scholes 2
David Seaman 7	Michael Owen 2
David Platt 7	Bobby Charlton 1
David Beckham 7	Geoff Hurst 1
Michael Owen 7	Ray Wilkins 1
Paul Scholes 7	Trevor Brooking 1
Paul Ince 7	Tony Woodcock 1
Steve McManaman 6	Bryan Robson 1
Martin Keown 6	Tony Adams 1
Gareth Southgate 6	
Gary Lineker 6	
Teddy Sheringham 5	
Kenny Sansom 5	
Phil Neville 5	
Darren Anderton 5	
Nicky Barmby 5	

The European Championship was originally called the UEFA European Nations Cup. The name change took place in 1968.

UEFA initially struggled to find 16 nations willing to compete, with no British Isles countries entering the first tournament.

Five European Championship finals have gone to extra-time (1960, 1968, 1976, 1996 and 2000). Only one has been decided on penalties – the 1976 final between West Germany and Czechoslovakia.

Peter Shilton is the oldest player to represent England at a European Championship. He was 38 years and 8 months old when he played against Holland in Dusseldorf during Euro 1988. This match also brought up his century of international caps.

Goalkeeper David Seaman was one of England's heroes of Euro 1996.

Gary Neville, England's most capped player at a European Championship, on the ball against Portugal at the 2000 tournament.

England's Record in European Championship Finals:

Played	Won	Drawn	Lost	For	Against
23	7	7	9	31	28

Did you know?
The largest attendance in European Championship history was for a qualifier between England and Scotland at Hampden Park for the 1968 competition. 130,711 fans crammed into the famous stadium.

England's skipper in 1996, Tony Adams, was solid and reliable in the centre of defence.

53

GERMANY

After analysing England's performances over the years, now it's time to study the opposition.

The nations on the following pages are some of the most successful in international football and many of them are great rivals of the Three Lions. There have been plenty of memorable encounters over the years, including penalty shoot-outs with Portugal, galling and glorious encounters against the Germans and fiesty-filled fixtures against Argentina.

"I always said and always believed we could beat Germany but I could not believe 5-1." – Sven-Goran Eriksson

Manager: Joachim Low
Most Appearances: Lothar Matthaus – 150
Highest Goalscorer: Gerd Muller – 68

Former German skipper, Lothar Matthaus, holds the record for the most appearances at the World Cup. The midfielder has played 25 times in the tournament.

The 2006 World Cup German squad included four players who were born outside Germany: Miroslav Klose and Lukas Podolski were born in Poland, Oliver Neuville in Switzerland and Gerald Asamoah hailed from Ghana.

League Table:

	Pl	W	D	L	GF	GA	GD	Pts
England	26	11	5	10	45	33	12	38
Germany	26	10	5	11	33	45	-12	35

Did you know?
Before the famous 5-1 thrashing by England in 2001, Germany had only ever lost one previous World Cup qualifying home match in their history. In the same game Michael Owen became the first England player to score a hat-trick against Germany since Geoff Hurst in 1966 when England won the World Cup.

Lothar Matthaus, Germany's record appearance holder, in action during the 1990 World Cup in Italy.

Honours:
World Cup: 1954, 1974, 1990
European Championship: 1972, 1980, 1996

First England Fixture: 10 May 1930
Last England Fixture: 22 August 2007

Steven Gerrard, flanked by Sol Campbell (left) and Ashley Cole (right), runs towards the England fans after scoring the second goal in the 5-1 thrashing of Germany in 2001.

ARGENTINA

Diego Maradona (right) skips round Peter Beardsley during the 1986 World Cup in Mexico.

Manager: Alfio Basile
Most Appearances: Javier Zanetti – 117
Highest Goalscorer: Gabriel Batistuta – 56

Juan Roman Riquelme (centre) shields the ball from Luke Young (left) and Ledley King (right) during a friendly in 2005.

Honours:
World Cup: 1978, 1986
Copa America: 1921, 1925, 1927, 1929, 1937, 1941, 1945, 1946, 1947, 1955, 1957, 1959, 1991, 1993

First England Fixture: 9 May 1951
Last England Fixture: 12 November 2005

League Table:

	Pl	W	D	L	GF	GA	GD	Pts
England	14	6	6	2	21	15	6	24
Argentina	14	2	6	6	15	21	-6	12

Argentina have won the Copa America an impressive 14 times. Their last success came in 1993.

In the 2006 World Cup, Argentina's Leandro Cufre was given a red card after the Quarter-final game with Germany had finished. He received his marching orders for his part in the brawl after the match, even though he was a substitute and had not participated in the game itself. It's the only time a player has been sent off in a World Cup after the final whistle.

Did you know?
Argentina have participated in four World Cup
Finals, winning two, in 1978 and 1986, and losing
two in 1930 and 1990.

Four years after being sent-off during the knock-out stage of France 1988, David Beckham (centre) has his revenge, slamming home England's winner in the 1-0 victory over Argentina at the 2002 World Cup.

HOLLAND

Manager: Marco Van Basten
Most Appearances: Edwin Van Der Saar – 121
Highest Goalscorer: Patrick Kluivert – 40

Holland's Ronald De Boer is put under pressure from Paul Ince at Euro 1996.

Holland coach Marco Van Basten, on the ball for the Dutch during his playing days.

Honours:
European Championship: 1988

First England Fixture: 18 May 1935
Last England Fixture: 15 November 2006

League Table:

	Pl	W	D	L	GF	GA	GD	Pts
England	17	5	8	4	24	19	5	23
Holland	17	4	8	5	19	24	-5	20

Holland reached the final of the 1974 and 1978 World Cups but were beaten on both occasions by countries hosting the tournament – West Germany in 1974 and Argentina in 1978.

Holland's record victory was a 9-0 thrashing of Norway in Rotterdam in 1972.

Alan Shearer slots in a penalty to open the scoring in 1996.

Did you know? International strikers Ruud Van Nistelrooy and Patrick Kluivert were born on the same day of the same year. Their shared date of birth is 1 July 1976.

Jaap Stam (right) and Andy Cole challenge for the ball during the 2001 match at White Hart Lane.

SCOTLAND

Scotland's joint record goalscorer, Kenny Dalglish, in action for the Tartan Army.

Manager: George Burley
Most Appearances: Kenny Dalglish – 102
Highest Goalscorers: Denis Law and
Kenny Dalglish – 30

Paul Scholes jumps highest to give England a 2-0 lead during the 1999 European Championship play-off match

Honours:
None.

First England Fixture: 30 November 1872
Last England Fixture: 17 November 1999

League Table:

	Pl	W	D	L	GF	GA	GD	Pts
England	110	45	24	41	192	169	23	159
Scotland	110	41	24	45	169	192	-23	147

England played Scotland in the first ever international football match on Saturday 30 November 1872. The game was played at the West of Scotland Cricket Ground in Glasgow and the score ended 0-0.

Scotland have qualified for the World Cup Finals on eight occasions but have never gone further than the first round.

Hughie Gallacher holds the record for most goals scored in one Scotland match. Gallacher scored five goals in the 7–3 win against Northern Ireland in February 1929.

Did you know?
Scotland's record victory came in 1901 when they beat Ireland 11-0 in the Home Championship fixture.

"Scotland have a mountain to climb, but if there's one team that is used to that, it's them. There are a lot of mountains around Scotland." – Kevin Keegan following England's 2-0 play-off first leg victory in 1999

Scotland skipper Gary McAllister holds his head in disbelief after David Seaman's spectacular penalty save in 1996.

Brazil's best player and record goalscoer, the great Pelé.

BRAZIL

Manager: Dunga
Most Appearances: Cafu – 156
Highest Goalscorer: Pelé – 77

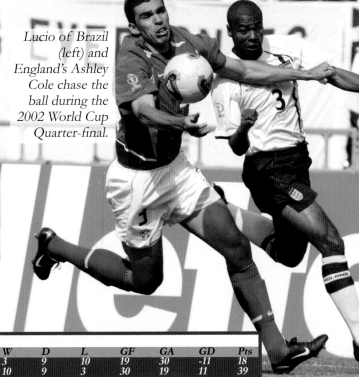

Lucio of Brazil (left) and England's Ashley Cole chase the ball during the 2002 World Cup Quarter-final.

Honours:
World Cup: 1958, 1962, 1970, 1994, 2002
Copa America: 1919, 1922, 1949, 1989, 1997, 1999, 2004, 2007
Confederations Cup: 1997, 2005

First England Fixture: 9 May 1956
Last England Fixture: 1 June 2007

League Table:

	Pl	W	D	L	GF	GA	GD	Pts
England	22	3	9	10	19	30	-11	18
Brazil	22	10	9	3	30	19	11	39

Brazil are the most successful national team in World Cup history. The Samba stars have won five tournaments and reached ten Semi-finals. They are the only country to participate in every single one of the 18 World Cups since the first tournament in 1930.

The Olympic football tournament is the only global international competition in football that Brazil have never won.

England's last meeting with Brazil at a major tournament was the Quarter-final of the 2002 World Cup. The Brazilians held on for a 2-1 victory, despite playing much of the second half with ten men following Ronaldinho's red card.

Ronaldinho (centre) skips away from Nicky Shorey (left) and England captain John Terry at Wembley in 2007.

"I hoped we'd do better 11 versus 10, but we were tired and Brazil were very good at keeping the ball. Once it was 2-1 we were not strong enough to come back. But, no regrets. We had a great opportunity to reach the Semi-final and we didn't take it." – Sven-Goran Eriksson

PORTUGAL

Luis Figo, Portugal's most capped player, assesses his options during the 2006 World Cup.

Manager: Luiz Felipe Scolari
Most Appearances: Luis Figo – 127
Highest Goalscorer: Pauleta – 47

Cristiano Ronaldo in full flow against England at Euro 2004.

Honours:
None.

First England Fixture: 25 May 1947
Last England Fixture: 1 July 2006

League Table:	Pl	W	D	L	GF	GA	GD	Pts
England	22	9	10	3	45	25	20	37
Portugal	22	3	10	9	25	45	-20	19

In the 2006 World Cup, Portugal set a record for the number of yellow cards received by a national team in a single World Cup, with a total of 24 bookings.

Portugal have knocked England out of the last two major tournaments: the 2006 World Cup and 2004 European Championship. On both occasions the Three Lions were defeated on penalty kicks.

Since the first World Cup in 1930, Portugal have only qualified for four World Cup tournaments.

Did you know?
Pauleta was the leading goal scorer in the 2006 World Cup qualifiers but only managed one goal in six games at the actual tournament.

Joy for Portugal and disbelief for England as another major tournament ends with penalty shoot-out defeat, this time at the 2006 World Cup in Germany.

FRANCE

Manager: Raymond Domenech
Most Appearances: Lilian Thuram – 137
Highest Goalscorer: Thierry Henry – 44

*Zinedine Zida
(below right) leav
Steven Gerra
trailing in his wa
during the Eu
2004 Group matc*

*Thierry Henry,
France's record
goalscorer on
international
duty.*

Honours:
World Cup: 1998
European Championships: 1984, 2000
Confederations Cup: 2001, 2003

First England Fixture: 10 May 1923
Last England Fixture: 13 June 2004

League Table:

	Pl	W	D	L	GF	GA	GD	Pts
England	26	16	4	6	65	32	33	52
France	26	6	4	16	32	65	-33	22

> *"It was a bit of a mugging and hard to take, but we move on to our next two games knowing we did ourselves proud apart from two minutes in injury time." – Michael Owen on the French turnaround in 2004*

Frank Lampard's opening goal for England against France in Euro 2004, put an end to the French team's clean sheet of 11 matches. The last time the French had conceded a goal was against Turkey in the Confederations Cup on 26 June 2003.

In the same match, England led 1-0 until the 90th minute when Zinedine Zidane scored the equaliser, before bagging the winner deep into stoppage time to leave the Three Lions shell-shocked.

Did you know? Les Bleus became the first national team to hold both the World Cup and European Championship crowns when they won the European title in 2000.

The French squad celebrate their 1998 World Cup victory.

SPAIN

Manager: Luis Aragones
Most Appearances: Andoni Zubizarreta – 126
Highest Goalscorer: Raul – 44

*Spain's record scorer,
Raul, on the attack on
the international arena.*

Honours:
European Championship: 1964

First England Fixture: 15 May 1929
Last England Fixture: 7 February 2007

*Gareth Barry (left) and Fernando Torres tussle for
possession during a friendly at Old Trafford in 2007.*

League Table:

	Pl	W	D	L	GF	GA	GD	Pts
England	21	11	3	7	38	22	16	36
Spain	21	7	3	11	22	38	-16	24

In spite of their impressive qualifying record for the World Cup, and the quality of their players, Spain have only once progressed further than the Quarter-final stage of the tournament – in 1950, when they reached the Semi-finals.

Spain became the first non-British side to beat England when they won 4-3 in a friendly in Madrid in 1929.

Spain's joint biggest defeat came against England in 1931 when they lost 7-1. The Spaniards lost by the same scoreline to Italy in 1928.

Nicky Butt (right) storms through the Spanish midfield as Pablo misses a tackle during the 2004 friendly.

Did you know?
Spain and Brazil shared the FIFA Fair Play Award at the 2006 World Cup.

Tony Adams (left) slides in to deny Jose Caminero during the Quarter-final tie at Euro 1996.

ENGLAND 4 WEST GERMANY 2

Captain, Bobby Moore, celebrates the win with his team-mates.

Re-live some of English football's proudest moments and greatest ever matches on the following pages.

The 1966 victory remains England's biggest football achievement to date...

"Some people are on the pitch... they think it's all over...it is now!"

BBC sports commentator Ken Wolstenholme will always be remembered for his famous line at the end of the 1966 World Cup Final

30 July 1966, Wembley

England: Banks, Cohen, Charlton J, Moore, Wilson, Ball, Stiles, Peters, Hunt, Charlton R, Hurst

"England's best football will come against the right type of opposition – a team who come to play football and not act like animals." –
Alf Ramsey reacting angrily to foul play in the Quarter-final against Argentina

Tournament details
Host nation: England
Dates: 11 July – 30 July
Teams: 16 (from 5 confederations)
Venue(s): 8 (in 7 host cities)
Champions: England (1 title)

Tournament statistics
Matches: 32
Goals scored: 89
(2.78 per match)
Attendance: 1,635,000
(51,094 per match)
Top scorer: Eusebio (9 goals)

Did you know?
The 1966 World Cup victory was ranked third of the 100 Greatest Sporting Moments in 2002 by Channel Four.

The 1966 World Cup winning team pose with the trophy.

"We were the champions, which was a fantastic feeling. I knew that life for me would never be the same again."
– Sir Bobby Charlton

ENGLAND 4 N IRELAND 0

7 February 1979, Wembley

England: Clemence, Neal, Watson, Hughes, Mills, Coppell, Currie, Brooking, Keegan, Latchford, Barnes

It had been 12 long years since England had fought their way through a qualifying group to reach the finals of a major tournament (they had been spared this as defending world champions in Mexico in 1970). Now there was a reasonable opportunity, because they had been drawn in a group with Denmark, Ireland, Northern Ireland and Bulgaria for a place in the European Championship. An exciting 4-3 victory in Copenhagen was followed by a gritty 1-1 draw in Dublin.

For the next game, Northern Ireland, managed by the legendary Danny Blanchflower, came to Wembley, packed with good players such as Pat Rice, Sammy Nelson, Martin O'Neill, Sammy McIlroy and Gerry Armstrong, and a world-class goalkeeper in Pat Jennings. They were not strangers to the odd win at Wembley.

England's nerves were steadied when Kevin Keegan got the vital goal during the opening half.

Did you know?
Apart from Sir Alf Ramsey, Kevin Keegan is the only man to have both captained and managed England.

Bob Latchford added a double in the second half, either side of a Dave Watson goal.

Kevin Keegan torments the Northern Ireland defence during the 1979 match-up.

Bob Latchford, who bagged a brace against Northern Ireland, on England duty.

ENGLAND 3 FRANCE 1

16 June 1982, Bilbao

England: Shilton, Mills, Thompson, Butcher, Sansom (Neal), Coppell, Robson, Wilkins, Rix, Mariner, Francis

This was England's first game in the finals of the World Cup since Mexico in 1970. Both the fans and players seemed nervous.

England had stuttered through their qualifying group, whereas the French, crammed with skilful ball players such as Michel Platini, Alain Giresse and Dominique Rocheteau, were making a name for themselves. It was vital for England to get a good start.

Within 27 seconds, Bryan Robson was hooking the ball into the net, and

Bryan Robson (top) heads home his second goal against France at the 1982 World Cup.

the massive English support in Bilbao erupted. However, France brushed this off and equalised within 25 minutes through Gerard Soler. The match remained tight and tense until half-time.

In the second half, Robson struck again. Now the French had to attack in even greater numbers, and their defence was exposed once more when Paul Mariner sealed the win seven minutes from the end.

Unfortunately, this proved to be the zenith of England's fortunes in Spain, as they crashed out in the next round. The luck of the draw favoured France, and they proceeded to the Semi-finals.

Paul Mariner (left) in action against Spain during the 1982 tournament.

Did you know?

Paul Mariner scored in the five consecutive England matches he played between 18 November 1982 and the World Cup tie with France on 16 June 1982. England's previous four opponents were Hungary, Holland, Scotland and Finland.

ENGLAND 3 POLAND 0

11 June 1986, Monterrey

England: Shilton, Stevens G, Butcher, Fenwick, Sansom, Steven, Hoddle, Reid, Hodge, Lineker (Dixon), Beardsley (Waddle)

It was now or never for England. Unless they beat Poland, they were almost certainly going out of the World Cup. The Poles, meanwhile, were definitely through to the next stage, whatever happened.

Manager Bobby Robson finally bowed to the inevitable and picked Peter Reid instead of his unfit namesake, skipper Bryan (his two injury-riddled games were to be repeated in the 1990 World Cup finals). With Trevor Steven replacing the banned Wilkins, the midfield was reshaped, largely around Glenn Hoddle.

Within the first ten minutes, Lineker had scored and, five minutes later, he achieved another goal. Unbelievably, ten minutes from the interval, he had a third. England, and this was unprecedented in a match in the World Cup finals, were cruising.

The second half was an anti-climax, but it didn't really matter. England were through to the last 16.

Having never won a game by three clear goals in any World Cup finals before, England promptly did it again against Paraguay, before meeting Maradona and Argentina.

Lineker was awarded the Golden Boot as the highest scorer, with six goals.

Gary Lineker in action for England during the 1986 World Cup in Mexico.

Did you know? Gary's magnificent finishing earned him 48 goals in 80 appearances, leaving him second only to Bobby Charlton on England's all-time list (by one goal).

ENGLAND 3 CAMEROON 2

1 July 1990, Naples

England: Shilton, Parker, Butcher (Steven), Walker, Wright, Pearce, Platt, Gascoigne, Waddle, Lineker, Barnes (Beardsley)

No one could claim that England were setting the World Cup finals alight – although, they were proving difficult to beat and adept at getting the right results when needed.

Cameroon, on the other hand, had been a revelation in Italy from the moment they had beaten defending champions Argentina in the opening game.

England began quite well and Platt secured the lead in the first half. But it was clear that Cameroon, the livelier side, were not out of the match at half-time. After bringing on Roger Milla, Cameroon turned the match on its head.

First Emmanuel Kunde slotted home a penalty, then Eugene Ekeke grabbed the lead almost as soon as he came on the pitch. Unless England could find a riposte, they were out.

Peter Shilton had to be at his best to make a save from Omam Biyik. Then, with seven minutes left, Lineker forced a penalty and he stepped up, the picture of concentration, and converted it to take the game into extra-time.

Cameroon still often appeared to be the more exuberant team, but their goalkeeper, Thomas Nkono, clumsily challenged Lineker, awarding England another penalty. Lineker slammed the ball down the middle of the goal and England were through to meet West Germany.

Gary Lineker was spot on against Cameroon at Italia 1990 as his two penalties sealed a 3-2 victory.

ENGLAND 2 SCOTLAND 0

15 June 1996, Wembley

England: Seaman, Neville G, Pearce (Redknapp) (Campbell), Adams, Southgate, Ince (Anderton), McManaman, Gascoigne, Anderton, Sheringham, Shearer

As a frustrating first half for the Three Lions came to an end, with the scores locked at 0-0, many England fans were concerned about their side's tournament chances. Scotland had battled well and enjoyed plenty of possession, defending stoutly and often out-numbering the English in midfield.

Terry Venables brought on a young Jamie Redknapp after the interval to get a grip of the game, and the Liverpool man's accurate passing played a major role in England taking charge.

The first goal came from a surging right-flank run from Gary Neville, whose deep cross was finished off by Alan Shearer's header. Scotland refused to give in and after 76 minutes they earned a penalty after a crude Tony Adams tackle on Gordon Durie.

Gary McAllister stepped up with the hopes of a nation on his shoulders, but half-way through his run up, the ball moved slightly on the penalty spot. He took the kick anyway and David Seaman pulled off a fantastic save to maintain England's lead.

Three minutes later, Gazza scored his memorable goal which sealed the win.

"England have the best fans in the world and Scotland's fans are second-to-none." – Kevin Keegan

Did you know?
Paul Gascoigne won 57 caps, scoring nine
memorable goals for England. A smooth passer
and highly accomplished dribbler, Gazza always
looked to attack and create something magical.

Gazza scores one of the greatest goals Wembley has ever witnessed to put England two goals ahead during Euro 1996.

ENGLAND 4 HOLLAND 1

18 June 1996, Wembley

England: Seaman, Neville G, Adams, Southgate, Pearce, McManaman, Gascoigne, Ince (Platt), Anderton, Shearer (Fowler), Sheringham (Barmby).

Scoring 30 goals in 63 games, Alan Shearer was possibly the last great exponent of traditional English centre-forward play, forging a classic partnership with Teddy Sheringham.

Even after various injuries had curtailed his pace, he was still able to act as a supreme target man and foil for strikers, such as Michael Owen. Shearer enjoyed a highly successful club career with Southampton, Blackburn Rovers and Newcastle United.

Teddy Sheringham guides home his second and England's fourth in the famous 4-1 victory over the Dutch at Euro 1996.

Alan Shearer almost breaks the net as he slams in England's third and best goal against Holland.

"If you can't stand the heat in the dressing room, get out of the kitchen." – Terry Venables

This was the final group game between two teams who had been expected to dominate and qualify for the 1996 Quarter-finals. But with a win and a draw each, neither England nor Holland had yet kicked into gear. That changed on a balmy summer night in London.

With just over 20 minutes gone, Shearer opened up the scores. There were rumours that the Dutch camp was split down the middle, and that manager Guus Hiddink was facing a players' rebellion. It did seem as if their team weren't responding in their usual manner, but at half-time, the score remained at 1-0.

However, in a glorious ten-minute spell soon after the interval, the floodgates opened. Sheringham scored, adding to Shearer's goal, then both Shearer and Sheringham scored again. It was technically advanced football played with stunning purpose.

The Wembley crowd had not seen a top-class side demolished in such style for years, and roared their approval. Terry Venables, a former manager of Barcelona, considered it the most vibrant atmosphere he had ever experienced.

Not even Patrick Kluivert's late consolation (which sneaked the shattered Dutch into the Quarter-finals) could spoil the party. Thirty years of hurt appeared to be at an end.

ENGLAND 5 GERMANY 1

When wins against Finland, Albania and Greece gave England an outside chance of recovering from their home defeat by Germany the previous year, this was the first massive test of Sven-Goran Eriksson's managerial reign. England simply had to win to have a chance of automatic qualification for the World Cup Finals – otherwise, a difficult play-off loomed ahead.

The game started badly for England. The physically imposing Carsten Jancker seized on a defensive mix-up after six minutes. But heads didn't drop, and barely six minutes later Nicky Barmby headed across goal for Michael Owen to hook in the equaliser.

1 September 2001, Munich

England: Seaman, Neville G, Ferdinand, Campbell, Cole A, Beckham, Scholes (Carragher), Gerrard (Hargreaves), Barmby (McManaman), Owen, Heskey

Things got even better as Owen ran their statuesque rearguard ragged and, after forcing a corner, Steven Gerrard cracked home a blistering second just on half-time.

If that was good, the second half was magical. Put through twice more, Owen finished with cool aplomb each time to notch a staggering hat-trick.

"To beat Germany, yes, okay, yet 5-1? It just doesn't happen." – Sven-Goran Eriksson

Not since England went to Berlin in 1938 and won 6-3 had Germany been so outclassed at home. Then Heskey swept in a fifth and everyone – players, managers and fans – reeled in a state of shock.

Michael Owen completes his hat-trick to put England 4-1 up in Munich.

ENGLAND 3 ARGENTINA 2

12 November 2005, Geneva

England: Robinson, Young (Crouch), Ferdinand, Terry, Bridge (Konchesky), Beckham, King (Cole J), Lampard, Gerrard, Owen, Rooney

Argentina came to Europe playing superbly, as they were to do throughout the 2006 World Cup in Germany. For once, a friendly match was taken extremely seriously, possibly because the neutral venue enhanced the World Cup rehearsal status.

Inspired by their outstanding playmaker, Juan Roman Riquelme, and his chief right-hand man, Maxi Rodriguez, Argentina played fast, flowing football.

After a slow start, Rooney equalised Hernan Crespo's opener in a sharp interchange of goals just before half-time.

In the second half, defender Walter Samuel came up to score and England looked to have fallen short as the belated round of substitutions began.

But Eriksson threw caution to the wind and brought on Peter Crouch for a defender, and the Argentinian back-four wilted.

The ensuing confusion was tailor-made for Owen who snapped up a brace of goals in the final minutes to turn the match on its head.

Did you know?
The game was a fitting match for Beckham's 50th as captain of England.

Joe Cole (foreground), Michael Owen and Wayne Rooney celebrate beating Argentina 3-2 in 2005.

MATTHEWS & FINNEY

There have been hundreds of great England players over the years, as the home of football has produced some of the world's finest goalkeepers, including Gordon Banks and Peter Shilton, classy defenders like Bobby Moore and Rio Ferdinand, marauding midfielders like Bobby Charlton and Bryan Robson, and lethal strikers such as Gary Lineker and Alan Shearer. The following pages concentrate on just a selection of great lions.

A supremely gifted and clever winger, Stanley Matthews was known as the 'wizard of dribble'. He was full of tricks and shimmies, and his forays down either flank had back-peddling full-backs in a daze, swinging at fresh air as they attempted to make a tackle.

Matthews is England's oldest ever goalscorer. He was 41 years and 248 days old when he struck against Northern Ireland in Belfast on 6 October 1956.

Stanley Matthews

Caps: 54
Goals: 11
Won: 32
Lost: 14
Drawn: 8
Debut: Vs Wales, 29 September 1934
Last game: Vs Denmark, 15 May 1957
Clubs: Stoke City, Blackpool

"He (Matthews) was the man who taught us how football should be played." – Pelé

"Tom Finney would have been great in any team, in any match and in any age ... even if he had been wearing an overcoat." – Bill Shankly

Sir Tom Finney was left-footed, but preferred to play on the right wing and, when on international duty, he could operate on either flank and often as a centre-forward. The Preston North End legend boasts an excellent goalscoring record for England, but he also created countless chances and goals for his team-mates.

Tom Finney (right) whips in one of his trademark crosses whilst playing for the Three Lions.

England's 'wizard of dribble', Stanley Matthews, torments the Scotland full-back.

Tom Finney

Caps: 76
Goals: 30
Won: 51
Lost: 12
Drawn: 13
Debut: Vs Ireland, 28 September 1946
Last game: Vs USSR, 22 October 1958
Club: Preston North End

WRIGHT & LOFTHOUSE

An influential skipper for club and country, Billy Wright was a commanding and uncompromising defender. The Wolves legend possessed excellent positional sense and was strong in the air and on the deck.

Billy Wright missed only three England games from the beginning to the end of his international career.

Captain Billy Wright leads England out to battle with Scotland in 1959.

Billy Wright

Caps: 105
Goals: 3
Won: 60
Lost: 21
Drawn: 24
Debut: Vs Ireland, 28 September 1946
Last game: Vs USA, 28 May 1959
Club: Wolverhampton Wanderers

Did you know?
Billy Wright managed Arsenal for
four seasons in the 1960s.

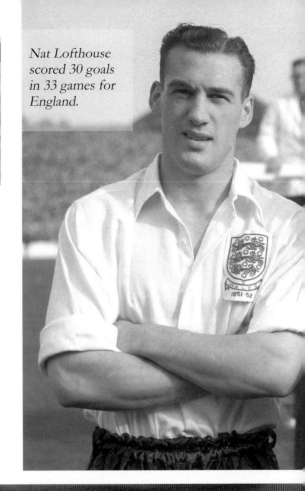

Nat Lofthouse scored 30 goals in 33 games for England.

Nat Lofthouse

Caps: 33
Goals: 30
Won: 16
Lost: 5
Drawn: 12
Debut: Vs Yugoslavia, 22 November 1950
Last game: Vs Wales, 26 November 1958
Club: Bolton Wanderers

Famously known as the 'Lion of Vienna', thanks to an inspiring performance for England against Austria when Lofthouse scored the winning goal in a 3-2 triumph, despite being injured. The Bolton centre-forward was aggressive and ultra-competitive but also a fine finisher, as his international record illustrates.

BALL & HUGHES

A terrier-like winger whose awesome energy levels were crucial to England's 1966 World Cup success, Alan Ball was an energetic midfielder with excellent passing ability. His pace, acceleration and natural balance allowed him to buzz past defenders and play dangerous balls into the box. Although playing more centrally in 1966, Ball's work ethic and desire to link up with the forwards gave England width when they needed it, as illustrated when he set up Geoff Hurst's second goal in the Final.

Emlyn Hughes

Caps: 62
Goals: 1
Won: 32
Lost: 10
Drawn: 20
Debut: Vs Holland, 5 November 1969
Last game: Vs Scotland, 24 May 1980
Clubs: Blackpool, Liverpool, Wolverhampton Wanderers, Rotherham United, Hull City, Mansfield Town, Swansea City

Famously known as 'Crazy Horse', after Liverpool's legendary manager Bill Shankly had given him the label, Emlyn Hughes was a hard-working, whole-hearted and versatile performer, equally adept playing in midfield or defence.

Alan Ball

Caps: 72
Goals: 8
Won: 45
Lost: 8
Drawn: 19
Debut: Vs Yugoslavia, 9 May 1965
Last game: Vs Scotland, 24 May 1975
Clubs: Blackpool, Everton, Arsenal, Southampton, Philadelphia Fury, Vancouver Whitecaps, Eastern AA, Bristol Rovers

Did you know?
Emlyn captained England on 23 occasions.

'Crazy Horse' aka Emlyn Hughes in possession of the ball for England.

"He (Hughes) was an absolute legend. When I went to Liverpool he was the main man. He was a wonderful player and a fantastic example to everyone. He was the best person to learn from and a larger than life character." – Graeme Souness

KEEGAN & BROOKING

Had Kevin Keegan played in a better England side, he would surely be remembered as one of the country's best. The hard-working striker was an excellent finisher and a dangerous attacking force, whose exploits at club level for Liverpool and German side SV Hamburg, led to plenty of trophies and a European Player of the Year Award.

Keegan played only 26 minutes of football at the World Cup Finals due to England's poor qualifying record during the 1970s and his injury before the 1982 tournament.

'Special K', Kevin Keegan celebrates scoring against Scotland at Wembley in 1979.

"My father was a miner and he worked down a mine." – Kevin Keegan

Kevin Keegan

Caps: 63
Goals: 21
Won: 34
Lost: 12
Drawn: 17
Debut: Vs Wales, 15 November 1972
Last game: Vs Spain, 5 July 1982
Clubs: Scunthorpe United. Liverpool, SV Hamburg, Southampton, Newcastle United, Blacktown City Demons

Caps: 47
Goals: 5
Won: 25
Lost: 8
Drawn: 14
Debut: Vs Portugal, 3 April 1974
Last game: Vs Spain, 5 July 1982
Club: West Ham United

Did you know?
Trevor won The FA Cup with West Ham twice and scored the winning goal in the 1980 victory over Arsenal.

After Sir Bobby Charlton, Sir Trevor Brooking is the gentleman of English football. Like Kevin Keegan, he endured a somewhat frustrating international career. Brooking's subtle and skilful style was not typically English. He was two-footed, could pass and control the ball with accuracy, and had the happy knack of scoring vital goals.

Trevor Brooking in action against the Scots at Hampden Park.

ROBSON & BUTCHER

Christened 'Captain Marvel' thanks to his inspirational performances as skipper for both club and country, Bryan Robson always led by example at the heart of England's midfield, putting his body on the line, crunching into tackles and winning headers as part of his box-to-box, all-action style. 'Robbo' had a silky left foot and was an expert at arriving late in the box to score important goals.

Bryan Robson

Caps: 90
Goals: 26
Won: 46
Lost: 17
Drawn: 27
Debut: Vs Republic of Ireland, 6 February 1980
Last game: Vs Turkey, 16 October 1991
Clubs: West Bromwich Albion, Manchester United, Middlesbrough

"The real pity is that the England teams I played for didn't fulfil their potential. At the 1982 World Cup I was still comparatively young and learning the international game. Then, when I was at my peak and perhaps could have had an influence on tournaments, I had injuries. We certainly had the ability, individually and collectively, to achieve more than we did. I'm convinced the team we had in 1990, especially, was good enough to have won the World Cup." –
Bryan Robson

Bryan Robson, in action against Tunisia in 1990, was one of the finest all-round midfielders ever to play for England.

One of the hardest men to have performed in the England shirt, a shirt he famously once wore almost completely stained in his own blood, Terry Butcher was born to defend and could dominate even the most talented strikers in world football. Uncompromising in the challenge and an excellent man-marker, Butcher bludgeoned most of his opponents into submission before they got near the England goal.

Terry Butcher

Caps: 77
Goals: 3
Won: 45
Lost: 10
Drawn: 22
Debut: Vs Australia, 31 May 1980
Last game: Vs West Germany, 4 July 1990
Clubs: Ipswich Town, Glasgow Rangers, Coventry City, Sunderland

WADDLE & BEARDSLEY

The Geordie genius, Chris Waddle, often appeared ungainly and awkward on the football pitch. That was until he received the ball. Waddle was technically gifted and could play on either wing, using his distinctive dribbling style, which included a deceptive drop of the shoulder to create space for his accurate crosses. Waddle was also a free-kick specialist.

Chris Waddle prepares to take on another opponent whilst on England duty.

Chris Waddle

Caps: 62
Goals: 6
Won: 29
Lost: 11
Drawn: 22
Debut: Vs Republic of Ireland, 26 March 1985
Last game: Vs Turkey, 16 October 1991
Clubs: Newcastle United, Tottenham Hotspur, Olympic Marseille, Sheffield Wednesday, Falkirk, Bradford City, Sunderland, Burnley, Torquay United

Peter Beardsley

Caps: 59
Goals: 9
Won: 30
Lost: 8
Drawn: 21
Debut: Vs Egypt, 29 January 1986
Last game: Vs China, 23 May 1996
Clubs: Carlisle United, Vancouver Whitecaps, Manchester United, Newcastle United, Liverpool, Everton, Bolton Wanderers, Manchester City, Fulham, Hartlepool United, Melbourne Knights, Doncaster Rovers

A clever striker, who expertly operated in the deep-lying role, linking the midfield to the attack, Peter Beardsley played a major role in England's successful World Cup campaigns in 1986 and 1990. His insightful movement, passing ability and creative vision allowed Gary Lineker to flourish in the centre-forward role in front of him.

Peter Beardsley was a vital part of the 1986 and 1990 World Cup sides.

PEARCE & PLATT

Whole-hearted, unflinching in the tackle and a tiger-ish competitor, Stuart Pearce's presence in the England defence provided extra bite and a superb natural balance. The Nottingham Forest legend, whose famously known as 'Psycho', possessed a wickedly powerful left-foot shot and was one of the proudest men to have ever worn the Three Lions on his chest.

Stuart Pearce
Caps: 78
Goals: 5
Won: 40
Lost: 6
Drawn: 32
Debut: Vs Brazil, 19 May 1987
Last game: Vs Poland, 8 September 1999
Clubs: Wealdstone, Coventry City, Nottingham Forest, Newcastle United, West Ham United, Manchester City

Stuart Pearce clears the danger for the Three Lions with typical gusto during a friendly with Hungary at Wembley.

David Platt

Caps: 62
Goals: 27
Won: 29
Lost: 9
Drawn: 24
Debut: Vs Italy, 15 November 1989
Last game: Vs Germany, 26 June 1996
Clubs: Crewe Alexandra, Aston Villa, Bari,
Juventus, Sampdoria, Arsenal, Nottingham Forest

Despite Paul Gascoigne being the undisputed star of England's Italia 1990 World Cup campaign, David Platt's contribution to the Three Lion's success was just as telling. The former Aston Villa man weighed in with plenty of vital goals from midfield, including a classic volleyed winner in extra-time against Belgium in the knock-out stage. Platt captained his country on several occasions and produced a level of consistency in an England shirt that many players could only dream of.

David Platt celebrates yet another goal for England, on this occasion in 1991 against Argentina.

101

SHEARER & SHERINGHAM

Shearer was one of the most powerful and purposeful strikers to play for England. He expertly led the line, using his physical presence and hold-up play. Shearer was excellent in the air and a lethal finisher in front of the goal. The Geordie legend also captained his country on 34 occasions.

Alan Shearer

Caps: 63
Goals: 30
Won: 28
Lost: 13
Drawn: 22
Debut: Vs France, 19 February 1992
Last game: Vs Romania, 20 June 2000
Clubs: Southampton, Blackburn Rovers, Newcastle United

Power, pace and a deadly kick – Alan Shearer had everything a striker needed.

Did you know?
Alan Shearer missed only one of the penalties he took for England. His effort against Poland on 31 May in 1997 crashed back off the post.

Did you know?
Teddy notched the fastest goal
scored by an England substitute
when he hit the target against
Greece at Old Trafford on
6 October 2001.

The perfect foil for Alan Shearer in England's impressive Euro 1996 side, Teddy Sheringham's subtle skills and intelligent link-up play were crucial to England's success. A superb finisher in his own right, Sheringham's superb fitness levels ensured he was still impressing in an England shirt well into his 30s.

The perfect foil for Alan Shearer up
front, Teddy Sheringham in action
against Nigeria at the 2002 World Cup.

MANAGER RECORDS

England's first ever manager, Walter Winterbottom, on the training field.

Check out England's vital statistics over the next few pages and find out which England manager has the best win percentage, the oldest players to wear the shirt and some interesting facts about the England elevens.

England Managers

Manager	Reign
Walter Winterbottom	1946-1962
Sir Alf Ramsey	1963-1974
Joe Mercer	1974 (caretaker manager)
Don Revie	1974-1977
Ron Greenwood	1977-1982
Sir Bobby Robson	1982-1990
Graham Taylor	1990-1993
Terry Venables	1994-1996
Glenn Hoddle	1996-1999
Howard Wilkinson	1999 and 2000 (two separate occasions as caretaker manager)
Kevin Keegan	1999-2000
Peter Taylor	2000 (caretaker manager)
Sven-Goran Eriksson	2001-2006
Steve McClaren	2006-2007
Fabio Capello	2007 to present

"If you want to win football games, you've got to score goals." – Graham Taylor

Manager	Games	Won	Drawn	Lost	GF	GA	Win %
Walter Winterbottom	138	77	38	23	380	195	55.8%
Sir Alf Ramsey	113	69	27	17	224	98	61.1%
Joe Mercer	7	3	3	1	9	7	42.9%
Don Revie	29	14	8	7	49	25	48.3%
Ron Greenwood	55	33	12	10	93	40	60%
Sir Bobby Robson	95	47	30	18	154	60	49.5%
Graham Taylor	38	18	13	7	62	32	47.4%
Terry Venables	23	11	11	1	35	13	45.8%
Glenn Hoddle	28	17	6	5	42	13	60.7%
Howard Wilkinson	2	0	1	1	0	2	0%
Kevin Keegan	18	7	7	4	26	15	38.9%
Peter Taylor	1	0	0	1	0	1	0%
Sven-Goran Eriksson	67	40	17	10	128	61	59.7%
Steve McClaren	18	9	4	5	32	12	50%
Fabio Capello	1	1	0	0	2	1	100%

"I'm a firm believer that if the other side scores first you have to score twice to win." – Howard Wilkinson

Sven-Goran Eriksson looks for inspiration from above during the 2006 World Cup.

ALL-TIME RECORDS

Player Profile

Peter Shilton
Caps: 125
Goals: 0
Won: 66
Lost: 24
Drawn: 35
Debut: Vs East Germany, 25 November 1970
Last game: Vs Italy, 7 July 1990
Clubs: Leicester City, Stoke City, Nottingham Forest, Southampton, Derby County, Plymouth Argyle, Wimbledon, Bolton Wanderers, Coventry City, West Ham United, Leyton Orient

Top 20 England Appearances

1	Peter Shilton	125
2	Bobby Moore	108
3	Bobby Charlton	106
4	Billy Wright	105
5	David Beckham	100
6	Bryan Robson	90
7	Michael Owen	89
8	Kenny Sansom	86
9	Gary Neville	85
10	Ray Wilkins	84
11	Gary Lineker	80
12	John Barnes	79
13	Stuart Pearce	78
14	Terry Butcher	77
15	Tom Finney	76
16	David Seaman	75
17	Gordon Banks	73
18	Sol Campbell	73
19	Alan Ball	72
20	Martin Peters	67

One of the game's greatest goalkeepers, Peter Shilton's awesome ability was matched by his longevity. He played 1,390 times for 11 clubs during his career, finally calling it a day well into his late forties. 'Shilts' was a brilliant shot-stopper, dominated his area and possessed reliable handling and distribution. In his 125 games between the sticks, he conceded only 80 goals, and kept a record 65 clean sheets.

England's record victory was a 13-0 thrashing of Ireland in Belfast on 18 February 1882.

The Three Lions' record defeat came on 23 May 1954 when they were humbled 7-1 by Hungary in Budapest.

Top England 20 All Time Goal Scorers

No	Player	Goals	Games	Strike Rate
1	Bobby Charlton	49	106	0.46
2	Gary Lineker	48	80	0.60
3	Jimmy Greaves	44	57	0.77
4	Michael Owen	40	89	0.45
5	Tom Finney	30	76	0.39
6	Nat Lofthouse	30	33	0.91
7	Alan Shearer	30	63	0.48
8	Vivian Woodward	29	23	1.26
9	Steve Bloomer	28	23	1.22
10	David Platt	27	62	0.44
11	Bryan Robson	26	90	0.29
12	Geoff Hurst	24	49	0.49
13	Stan Mortensen	23	25	0.92
14	Tommy Lawton	22	23	0.96
15	Kevin Keegan	21	63	0.33
16	Mick Channon	21	46	0.46
17	Martin Peters	20	67	0.30
18	Johnny Haynes	18	56	0.32
19	Roger Hunt	18	34	0.53
20	Dixie Dean	18	16	1.13

Did you know?
Dixie Dean's scoring record in his first five England games was 2, 3, 2, 2, 3.

Tommy Lawton scored England's fastest goal when he netted after just 17 seconds in 1947.

England's record victory at Wembley was the 9-0 hammering dished out to Luxembourg on 15 December 1982.

DON'T QUOTE ME

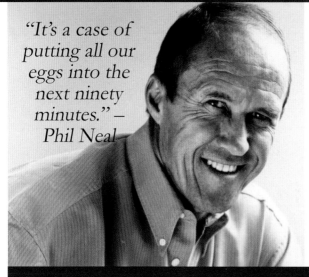

"It's a case of putting all our eggs into the next ninety minutes." – Phil Neal

"We keep kicking ourselves in the foot." – Ray Wilkins

"Hoddle hasn't been the Hoddle we know. Neither has Robson." – Ron Greenwood

"David Beckham's sending off cost us dearly. It was a mistake. But these things happen in football. I am not denying it cost us the game." – Glenn Hoddle

Players Sent Off while Playing for England:

Alan Mullery	Vs Yugoslavia	5 June 1968
Alan Ball	Vs Poland	6 June 1973
Trevor Cherry	Vs Argentina	12 June 1977
Ray Wilkins	Vs Morocco	6 June 1986
David Beckham	Vs Argentina	30 June 1998
Paul Ince	Vs Sweden	5 September 1998
Paul Scholes	Vs Sweden	5 June 1999
David Batty	Vs Poland	8 September 1999
Alan Smith	Vs Macedonia	16 October 2002
David Beckham	Vs Austria	8 October 2005
Wayne Rooney	Vs Portugal	1 July 2006

"Very few of us
have any idea
whatsoever of
what life is like
living in a goldfish
bowl, except,
of course, for
those of us who
are goldfish. "
Graham Taylor

"People always remember the second half."
Graham Taylor

109

FACTS & STATS

Englishmen Playing Abroad XI

1. Chris Woods	Glasgow Rangers
2. Gary Stevens	Glasgow Rangers
3. Owen Hargreaves	Bayern Munich
4. Des Walker	Sampdoria
5. Jonathan Woodgate	Real Madrid
6. Ray Wilkins	AC Milan
7. David Platt	Bari, Juventus, Sampdoria
8. Paul Gascoigne	Lazio, Glasgow Rangers
9. Gary Lineker	Barcelona
10. Trevor Francis	Sampdoria
11. Steve McManaman	Real Madrid

A star of England's Euro 1996 campaign who also impressed playing in Spain with Real Madrid, Steve McManaman is one of the most successful Englishmen to ply their trade abroad.

Did you know? Three father and son combinations have represented England. They are George Eastham Senior and George Eastham Junior, Brian Clough and Nigel Clough and Frank Lampard Senior and Frank Lampard Junior.

England Elevens:

All-Time England XI

1. Gordon Banks
2. Gary Neville
3. Stuart Pearce
4. Bryan Robson
5. Duncan Edwards
6. Bobby Moore
7. Alan Ball
8. Paul Gascoigne
9. Gary Lineker
10. Jimmy Greaves
11. Bobby Charlton

Did you know?
In a friendly with Holland in 1988 Tony Adams
was on the scoresheet for both sides.

Duncan Edwards, widely
regarded as one of England's
finest performers, despite only
making 18 appearances due to
his tragic and untimely death.

The Best Uncapped England XI

1. Tony Coton
2. Paul Elliot
3. Julian Dicks
4. Billy Bonds
5. Steve Bruce
6. Kevin Nolan
7. Jimmy Case
8. Rod Wallace
9. Mark Bright
10. Kevin Campbell
11. Howard Kendall

One-Cap Wonders XI

1. Nigel Spink
2. John Hollins
3. Steve Guppy
4. David Unsworth
5. Anthony Gardner
6. David Dunn
7. Lee Bowyer
8. Danny Wallace
9. Francis Jeffers
10. Chris Sutton
11. Mark Walters

*"It was a game we should have won.
We lost it because we thought we
were going to win it. But then again,
I thought that there was no way we
were going to get a result there." –
Jack Charlton*

Did you know?
When Owen Hargreaves was on the books at
Bayern Munich he won a full England cap without ever
having played for an English league club.

PLAYERS/MANAGERS

Glenn Hoddle was successful as a player and manager for England.

Did you know? England's longest unbeaten run was 20 matches and took place from 1889 to 1896.

Caps	Games	Won	Win %	Games Managed	Games Won	Win %
Alf Ramsey	32	18	56.3%	113	69	61.1%
Joe Mercer	5	3	60%	7	3	42.9%
Don Revie	6	3	50%	29	14	48.3%
Bobby Robson	20	11	55%	95	47	49.5%
Terry Venables	2	0	0%	23	11	47.8%
Glenn Hoddle	53	27	50.9%	28	17	60.7%
Kevin Keegan	63	34	53.9%	18	7	38.9%
Peter Taylor	4	3	75%	1	0	0%

"When a player gets to 30, so does his body." – Glenn Hoddle

Top Ten Oldest England Players	
1	Stanley Matthews aged 42 years, 102 days on 15 May 1957 v Denmark, WC Qualifier
2	Alexander Morten aged 41 years, 114 days on 8 Mar 1873 v Scotland, Friendly
3	Peter Shilton aged 40 years, 292 days on 7 Jul 1990 v Italy, World Cup
4	Frank Osborne aged 39 years, 221 days on 24 May 1926 v Belgium, Friendly
5	Edward Taylor aged 39 years, 40 days on 17 April 1926 v Scotland, Home Champ
6	David Seaman aged 39 years, 27 days on 16 October 2002 v Macedonia, EC Qualifier
7	Leslie Compton aged 38 years, 70 days on 22 November 1950 v Yugoslavia, Friendly
8	Stuart Pearce aged 37 years, 137 days on 8 September 1999 v Poland, EC Qualifier
9	Jesse Pennington aged 36 years, 230 days on 10 April 1920 v Scotland, Home Champ
10	Sam Hardy aged 36 years, 227 days on 10 Apr 1920 v Scotland, Home Champ

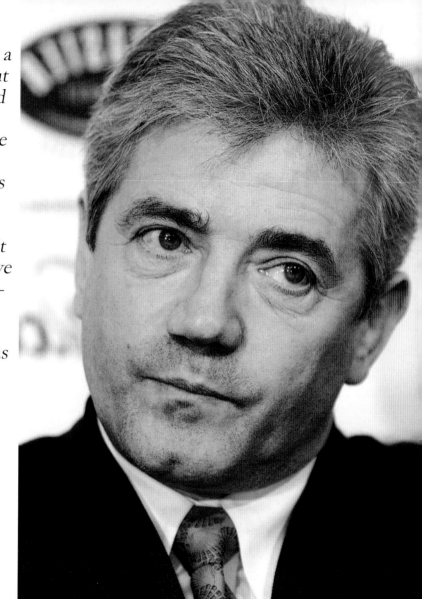

"I just feel I fall a little short about what is required in this job. I sat there in the first half and could see things weren't going right but I couldn't find it in myself to solve the problem." – Kevin Keegan announcing his resignation as England boss

BOBBY CHARLTON

Caps: 106
Goals: 49
Won: 60
Lost: 22
Drawn: 24
Debut: Vs Scotland, 19 April 1958
Last game: Vs West Germany, 14 June 1970
Clubs: Manchester United, Preston North End

The driving force of the England team throughout the 1960s, Bobby Charlton could hit a ball with great power using either foot and was a tireless worker playing in an advanced midfield role. The Manchester United legend scored plenty of vital goals for his country including some crucial strikes during the 1966 World Cup.

Bobby lets fly in typical fashion against Brazil at the 1970 World Cup.

Did you know?
Bobby was named European Footballer of the Year in 1966 following England's World Cup win.

Date	Opposition	Venue	Score	Bobby's Goals
19 April 1958	Scotland	Hampden Park	4-0	1
7 May 1958	Portugal	Wembley	2-1	2
4 October 1958	Northern Ireland	Windsor Park	3-3	2
22 October 1958	USSR	Wembley	5-0	1
11 April 1959	Scotland	Wembley	1-0	1
6 May 1959	Italy	Wembley	2-2	1
28 May 1959	USA	Wrigley Field	8-1	3
28 October 1959	Sweden	Wembley	2-3	1
9 April 1960	Scotland	Hampden Park	1-1	1
8 October 1960	Northern Ireland	Windsor Park	5-2	1
19 October 1960	Luxembourg	Municipal	9-0	3
23 November 1960	Wales	Wembley	5-1	1
10 May 1961	Mexico	Wembley	8-0	3
28 September 1961	Luxembourg	Highbury	4-1	2
22 November 1961	Northern Ireland	Wembley	1-1	1
2 June 1962	Argentina	Braden Cooper	3-1	1
29 May 1963	Czechoslovakia	Tehelne pole	4-2	1
2 June 1963	East Germany	Zentral Leipzig	2-1	1
5 June 1963	Switzerland	Sankt Jakob	8-1	3
12 October 1963	Wales	Ninian Park	4-0	1
17 May 1964	Portugal	Nacional	4-3	1
27 May 1964	USA	Downing	10-0	1
10 April 1965	Scotland	Wembley	2-2	1
20 October 1965	Austria	Wembley	2-3	1
2 April 1966	Scotland	Hampden Park	4-3	1
4 May 1966	Yugoslavia	Wembley	2-0	1
16 July 1966	Mexico	Wembley	2-0	1
26 July 1966	Portugal	Wembley	2-1	2
16 November 1966	Wales	Wembley	5-1	1
21 October 1967	Wales	Ninian Park	3-0	1
22 November 1967	Northern Ireland	Wembley	2-0	1
3 April 1968	Spain	Wembley	1-0	1
22 May 1968	Sweden	Wembley	3-1	1
8 June 1968	USSR	Olimpico, Rome	2-0	1
7 May 1969	Wales	Wembley	2-1	1
21 April 1970	Northern Ireland	Wembley	3-1	1
20 May 1970	Colombia	Nemesio Camacho	4-0	1

GARY LINEKER

Caps: 80
Goals: 48
Won: 39
Lost: 29
Drawn: 12
Debut: Vs Scotland, 26 May 1984
Last game: Vs Sweden, 17 June 1992
Clubs: Leicester City, Everton, Barcelona,
Tottenham Hotspur, Grampus Eight

A hero for his country and a reliable scorer for all his clubs, Gary Lineker was a gentleman on and off the pitch.

Gary Lineker was another predatory striker who was lethal in the six-yard box and always seemed to pop up with a vital goal exactly when England needed it most. His international total includes five hat-tricks and he is one of only three England players, along with Steve Bloomer and Jimmy Greaves, to have scored four goals in an England match twice. He will be remembered for the ten-goal total he scored at the 1986 and 1990 World Cups and for never being booked or sent off during his career.

Did you know?
Gary only ever missed one penalty for England. It came in a friendly against Brazil at Wembley in 1992. Had he hit the back of the net he would have ended as England's joint top scorer with Bobby Charlton.

Date	Opposition	Venue	Score	Gary's Goals
26 March 1985	Rep of Ireland	Wembley	2-1	1
16 June 1985	USA	Memorial Coliseum	5-0	2
16 October 1985	Turkey	Wembley	5-0	3
11 June 1986	Poland	Universitario	3-0	3
18 June 1986	Paraguay	Azteca	3-0	2
22 June 1986	Argentina	Azteca	1-2	1
15 October 1986	Northern Ireland	Wembley	3-0	2
18 February 1987	Spain	Bernabeu Stadium	4-2	4
19 May 1987	Brazil	Wembley	1-1	1
9 September 1987	West Germany	Rheinstadion	1-3	1
14 October 1987	Turkey	Wembley	8-0	3
23 March 1988	Holland	Wembley	2-2	1
24 May 1988	Colombia	Wembley	1-1	1
28 May 1988	Switzerland	Olympique	1-0	1
26 April 1989	Albania	Wembley	5-0	1
3 June 1989	Poland	Wembley	3-0	1
7 June 1989	Denmark	Idraetspark	1-1	1
28 March 1990	Brazil	Wembley	1-0	1
15 May 1990	Denmark	Wembley	1-0	1
11 June 1990	Rep of Ireland	Renato St Elia	1-1	1
1 July 1990	Cameroon	San Paolo	3-2	2
4 July 1990	West Germany	Stadio delle Alpi	1-1	1
12 September 1990	Hungary	Wembley	1-0	1
17 October 1990	Poland	Wembley	2-0	1
6 February 1991	Cameroon	Wembley	2-0	2
25 May 1991	Argentina	Wembley	2-2	1
3 June 1991	New Zealand	Mount Smart	1-0	1
12 June 1991	Malaysia	Merdeka	4-2	4
13 November 1991	Poland	Lech, Poznan	1-1	1
19 February 1992	France	Wembley	2-0	1
29 April 1992	CIS	Central, Moscow	2-2	1

JIMMY GREAVES

Caps: 57
Goals: 44
Won: 30
Lost: 14
Drawn: 13
Debut: Vs Peru, 17 May 1959
Last game: Vs Austria, 17 May 1967
Clubs: Chelsea, AC Milan, Tottenham Hotspur, West Ham United, Brentwood Town, Chelmsford City, Barnet

When Jimmy Greaves played for England, he usually scored, amassing a hugely impressive tally of 44 goals in 57 games, including six hat-tricks – a record that still stands.

Jimmy famously missed the 1966 Final after an injury earlier in the tournament ruled him out of the later stages and Geoff Hurst's fine form kept him out of the final. Probably England's most naturally talented striker and a deadly finisher, Jimmy Greaves is certainly one of the greats.

A natural born finisher, Jimmy Greaves had an excellent goalscoring record for England.

Date	Opposition	Venue	Score	Jimmy's Goals
17 May 1959	Peru	Nacional	1-4	1
17 October 1959	Wales	Ninian Park	1-1	1
11 May 1960	Yugoslavia	Wembley	3-3	1
8 October 1960	Northern Ireland	Windsor Park	5-2	2
19 October 1960	Luxembourg	Municipal	9-0	3
26 October 1960	Spain	Wembley	4-2	1
23 November 1960	Wales	Wembley	5-1	2
15 April 1961	Scotland	Wembley	9-3	3
24 May 1961	Italy	Olimpico, Rome	3-2	1
27 May 1961	Austria	Wiener, Prater	1-3	1
20 May 1962	Peru	Nacional, Lima	4-0	3
2 June 1962	Argentina	Braden Copper	3-1	1
20 October 1962	Northern Ireland	Windsor Park	3-1	1
21 November 1962	Wales	Wembley	4-0	1
29 May 1963	Czechoslovakia	Tehelne pole	4-2	2
12 October 1963	Wales	Ninian Park	4-0	1
23 October 1963	Rest of World	Wembley	2-1	1
20 November 1963	Northern Ireland	Wembley	8-3	4
24 May 1964	Rep of Ireland	Dalymount Park	3-1	1
30 May 1964	Brazil	Maracana	1-5	1
3 October 1964	Northern Ireland	Windsor Park	4-3	3
9 December 1964	Holland	Olympisch	1-1	1
10 April 1965	Scotland	Wembley	2-2	1
5 May 1965	Hungary	Wembley	1-0	1
4 May 1966	Yugoslavia	Wembley	2-0	1
29 June 1966	Norway	Ulleval	6-1	4
24 May 1967	Spain	Wembley	2-0	1

Did you know?
Jimmy Greaves played only three more games for
England after the 1966 World Cup finals, adding just
one further goal to his tally.

GLOSSARY

A – Away

AET – After Extra-time (as in the final score after extra-time)

D – Drawn

EC – European Championship

Euro – European Championship

FA – Football Association

FIFA – Fédération Internationale de Football (International Federation of Association Football)

GA – Goals Against

GD – Goal Difference

GF – Goals For

H – Home

Home Champ – Home Championship

Incl. – Including

International Debut – A player's first game for his country.

L – Lost

N Ireland – Northern Ireland

No. – Number

Pen(s) – Penalty-kick/ Penalties

Pld/Pl – Played
Pts – Points

Rep of Ireland – Republic of Ireland

SPAL – Societa Polisportiva Ars et Labor (an Italian football club)

Sub – Substitute

SV Hamburg – Sport-Verein Hamburg

UEFA - Union of European Football Associations

USSR – Union of Soviet Socialist Republics

V – Versus

Vs – Versus

W – Won

WC – World Cup

XI – Eleven

INDEX